The
Nancy Drew
Cookbook
Clues to Good Cooking
By Carolyn Keene

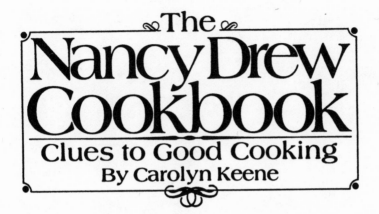

The Nancy Drew Cookbook
Clues to Good Cooking
By Carolyn Keene

Grosset & Dunlap
A Filmways Company
Publishers New York

1978 Printing

Library of Congress Catalog Card Number: 74-158753

ISBN: 0-448-02856-5 (Trade Edition)
ISBN: 0-448-03795-5 (Library Edition)

How can you become a really good cook?

"It's no mystery," Nancy Drew reveals. "You must do what fine cooks have always done—add your own special touch."

How do you do this? Let Nancy show you how. Who would be more intrigued to be an adventurer in cooking than a girl who loves to solve mysteries!

In this book she gives you over a hundred easy recipes and for some of them she has included her cooking secret. It may be a pinch of an herb, a secret sauce, a surprise cake. The trick can be anything that makes the food easier to prepare, tastier or more attractive-looking when served.

Of course, Nancy's friends have helped with her cookbook and Hannah Gruen has lent advice. Bess likes rich foods, George the slimming ones. The boys are the experts on barbecues, picnics and beach parties.

Nancy's acquaintances from overseas have sent recipes of their delicious native dishes, and there are surprise specialties even from Mr. Drew!

Just remember Nancy's two most important rules: follow the recipe carefully and add that little secret touch of hers. Or think up a mystery ingredient of your own!

Carolyn Keene

Carolyn Keene

CONTENTS

TO CLUE YOU IN

1. Unless you are an expert, follow the recipes exactly.

2. Put on an apron and wash your hands before starting to work.

3. Set out pot holders, utensils, and ingredients before beginning to prepare food.

4. Keep the handles of saucepans turned inward on the stove so they will not be knocked over.

5. Use a chopping board, instead of cutting directly on a table or counter top.

6. Never put rubber or plastic utensils in pots which are over heat—they will melt.

7. Place aluminum foil or a cookie sheet beneath the baking dish or on the oven rack to keep what you are cooking from dripping onto the oven bottom.

8. Before you use a hand beater or electric mixer, place a damp cloth beneath the mixing bowl. The cloth will keep the bowl from jiggling or "walking" on the counter or table top.

9. Get a clock with large, distinct markings so you can keep track of the minutes; or use a timer and set for desired length of time.

10. Make the quantities in measuring spoons and cups level, rather than heaped up.

11. Mix all liquid ingredients together. Then combine them with dry ingredients, pouring the liquid slowly into the dry ingredients and stirring.

12. Use a fork for stirring dry ingredients, particularly ground meat, and use a spoon for stirring liquids.

13. Grease baking dishes with wax paper or a paper towel dipped in butter, margarine, or cooking oil.

14. Use a cup or cream pitcher to transfer mixtures to muffin cups or freezer trays.

15. To prevent the discoloration of peeled apples, pears and peaches, sprinkle lemon juice over them; or soak them in pineapple or grapefruit juice.

16. Put onions under water while you peel them so that your eyes won't "cry."

17. Eggs can be tested for freshness by leaving them in cold water for a little while. If they rise to the top, they are bad!

18. Unless the recipe states differently, break the egg in half. Tap it against the sharp edge of a bowl just enough to crack the shell. Hold it over the bowl and with your fingers open the crack to let the whole egg drop into the bowl.

19. Use cold water to clean chocolate or egg from dishes.

20. When you have finished cooking, be sure that the oven, burners, and lights of the stove are turned off.

21. Always try to keep your kitchen clean and neat as you cook. Use only the dishes you will need. Measure ingredients on wax paper whenever possible. Wipe up any spills quickly.

Votes for Good Breakfasts

"Nancy Drew!" exclaimed Bess Marvin as she stopped short in the dining room door. "What in the world! Look at all the food!"

"It's a breakfast smorgasbord!" said George Fayne, Bess's tomboy cousin. The attractive girls had been invited to the Drew home for Saturday breakfast.

Nancy's blue eyes sparkled. "There are only twelve different dishes," she said. "I'm trying out these recipes for my cookbook."

As she spoke, the doorbell rang and Hannah Gruen, the Drews' housekeeper, hurried to open the front door. Deep masculine voices were heard.

"It's the boys!" said George, grinning. "Just wait till they see this!"

Moments later Ned Nickerson, Nancy's special friend, Dave Evans, Bess's steady date, and Burt Eddleton, George's friend, were staring speechless at the spread of colorful, delicious-smelling food.

"Wow!" exclaimed Ned with a twinkle in his eye. "Do you do this every day, Nancy?"

She laughed. "No. These dishes are not for busy mornings—just for weekends and holidays."

Just then Mr. Drew joined them, beaming.

"Now we'll test my daughter's recipes," he said, "and choose the best ones for her cookbook."

Everybody took a plate and forty minutes later they voted. The next week the test was repeated with twelve more dishes. In the following chapter are the recipes which won.

CHAPTER 1

Time for Breakfast

HOLLOW OAK NEST EGGS

TAPPING HEELS GRIDDLE CAKES

CHIEF MC GINNIS' WAFFLES

99 STEPS FRENCH TOAST

CRUMBLING WALL COFFEE CAKE

BLACKWOOD HALL MUFFINS

GEORGE'S "KEEP IN SHAPE"
GRAPEFRUIT

SKI JUMP HOT CHOCOLATE

HOLLOW OAK NEST EGGS

2   slices white bread (not too thin)
1   tablespoon cooking oil
2   eggs
Salt
Pepper

Dig out a "nest" in the center of each slice of bread.

Pour cooking oil in a medium-sized skillet and turn heat to medium.

Place the bread slices in the skillet. Brown them on one side and turn them over. Break the eggs and put one in the center of each slice. Sprinkle on salt and pepper. Turn the heat low and cook until the eggs have set—about 5 minutes.

Serves 2.

A HINT FROM NANCY

Buy uncut whole wheat bread for this recipe. Then you can make the slices as thick as you like.

TAPPING HEELS
GRIDDLE CAKES

½   cup milk
2   tablespoons melted butter
1   egg
1   cup flour
2   teaspoons baking powder
2   tablespoons sugar
½   teaspoon salt

Beat the milk, butter and egg lightly in a large bowl.

Sift the other ingredients together and add them to the liquid mixture. Stir just enough to dampen the flour. If necessary, add more milk to make the batter as thick as heavy cream.

Lightly grease griddle or skillet. Heat. Sprinkle a few drops of water on it. When the drops "dance" around, the pan is hot enough. Spoon the batter onto the pan. When bubbles start to form on a cake, flip it over with a pancake turner.

Makes 8 cakes.

CLUE TO EXTRA GOODNESS

Pour honey or maple syrup ¹₂-inch deep into a skillet and let it simmer. As the cakes are baked, ease them into the skillet. Cook 15 seconds on each side. Serve with a tablespoon of melted butter or margarine poured on top.

15

CHIEF MC GINNIS'S WAFFLES

2   eggs
2   cups flour
½   teaspoon salt
1½   cups milk
3   teaspoons baking powder
3   tablespoons melted butter

Heat the waffle iron.

Break eggs, putting the yolks in one mixing bowl and the whites in another. Beat the yolks well and add the milk.

Sift the flour, baking powder, and salt together. Gradually add the dry ingredients to the yolks and milk. Stir until the mixture is smooth. Add the melted butter and stir.

Beat the egg whites stiff and fold them into the mixture. (Use clean, dry beaters or egg whites will not froth.)

Spoon 3 tablespoons of batter on the iron and close it.

Bake for 5 minutes or until brown.

Makes 8 large waffles.

NANCY'S NUTRITION SECRET

Make a sauce for these waffles by mixing a tablespoon of lemon juice, ¹₂ cup of honey, and ⅔ cup of butter. Warm before pouring on the waffles.

99 STEPS FRENCH TOAST
(Don't worry—it's only a 3-step recipe!)

4   thin slices bread
1   egg
⅓   cup milk
1   teaspoon butter

Beat the egg until it is frothy. Add milk to the mixture and beat again.

Melt butter slowly in a skillet. Soak bread slices one by one in the egg mixture and lift them into the skillet with a pancake turner.

Brown on each side. Serve with maple syrup, confectioner's sugar, or cinnamon and sugar. Or try orange marmalade or apple butter on the French toast.

CRUMBLING WALL
COFFEE CAKE

1 ½   sticks (6 ounces) butter, melted
½   cup maple sugar
½   cup fine dry bread crumbs
1   egg
⅓   cup granulated sugar
⅓   cup milk
1   cup self-rising pancake mix

Heat the oven to 375°.

In a medium-sized bowl mix together ½ cup melted butter, maple sugar, and bread crumbs. Press the mixture against the bottom and sides of a 1-quart ring mold.

In another bowl break the egg and add the white sugar. Beat until fluffy. Add the milk and pancake mix to the egg-and-sugar mixture. Stir lightly until all ingredients are combined. Stir in 3 tablespoons of melted butter. Pour the entire mixture on top of the maple sugar mixture already in the ring mold.

Bake for 25 minutes. Let the cake cool 5 minutes before you turn it upside down on a warm platter and let it fall away from the mold. It tastes best when served warm.

A DETECTIVE NEEDS ENERGY

Add more protein to your cake by mixing ½ cup of finely chopped pecans to the maple sugar mixture.

18

BLACKWOOD HALL MUFFINS

1 ½	cups flour
½	cup sugar
2	teaspoons baking powder
½	teaspoon salt
4	tablespoons butter or margarine
1	egg
½	cup milk
1	cup fresh blueberries

Heat the oven to 400°.

Sift flour, sugar, baking powder, and salt into a mixing bowl.

Add the shortening, egg, and milk. Stir with a fork until blended.

Rinse blueberries and drain them on paper towels. Stir them into the dough until thoroughly mixed. Grease the bottom and sides of the muffin cups and fill ⅔ full with dough. Bake for 20 minutes. Muffins will be golden brown when done.

Makes 12 muffins.

FOR MYSTERIOUS FLAVOR

Substitute ¼ cup of soya flour for the same amount of regular flour and you'll add extra protein to your breakfast.

GEORGE'S "KEEP IN SHAPE" GRAPEFRUIT

1   grapefruit
Butter
1   tablespoon sugar
¼   teaspoon cinnamon
Maraschino cherries

Cut the grapefruit in half. Loosen fruit from skin, then cut each section close to the membrane. Remove the core. Dot each half with butter.

Combine sugar and cinnamon in a bowl and sprinkle it over the grapefruit halves. Put them on the broiler rack 4 inches from the heat. Cook for 8 minutes.

Decorate with maraschino cherries.

Serves 2.

NANCY SAYS

You can use this recipe as a dessert; substitute honey for the sugar-and-cinnamon mixture.

20

SKI JUMP HOT CHOCOLATE

4   squares unsweetened chocolate
1   cup sugar
½   cup water
2   teaspoons instant coffee
¼   teaspoon cinnamon
⅛   teaspoon salt
½   cup heavy whipping cream
2   quarts hot milk

Put chocolate, sugar, water, coffee, cinnamon, and salt into a saucepan. Stir them together over medium heat and bring the mixture to a boil. Then lower the heat and cook gently for 4 minutes, stirring the mixture constantly. Remove from the heat and let the mixture cool. Whip the cream with a hand beater or mixer. When the chocolate mixture has cooled, stir it into the whipped cream.

Put 2 tablespoons of the mixture into each cup. Fill the cups with hot milk. Stir before serving.

Serves 16.

STICKY SUGGESTION

Substitute 2 tablespoons of blackstrap molasses, a great energy booster, for the instant coffee.

BRUNCH FOR SLEEPYHEADS

PHANTOM EGGS
NANCY'S SCRAMBLER
GOLDEN PAVILION PINEAPPLE HAM
OLD STAGECOACH SAUSAGE LOAF
RIVER HEIGHTS FISH DISH
NED'S POTATO PANCAKES
HANNAH'S CHEESE PUFFS
RED GATE FARM TOMATOES
CAPTIVE BISCUITS

PHANTOM EGGS
(Now you see them, now you don't!)

5   eggs
1   can undiluted tomato soup
½   cup buttered bread crumbs
      (Melt 2 tablespoons of butter and mix crumbs into the butter until they are covered.)

Place the eggs in a saucepan and cover with cold water. When the water comes to a boil, lower heat and simmer for 15 minutes. Let the hard-boiled eggs stand in cold water a few minutes, and peel them. Slice each into 5 or 6 pieces.

Heat the oven to 400°.

Rub the bottom and sides of a baking dish with softened butter or margarine. Cover the bottom of the dish with egg slices. Spoon tomato soup over the egg slices. Make layers of egg slices covered with soup until you have used up the eggs. Spread buttered bread crumbs on the top of the dish. Bake for 20 minutes.

Serves 5.

NANCY'S NUTRITION HINT

At times Nancy chops 2 tablespoons of green pepper and sprinkles some over each layer of eggs and soup. This adds color as well as vitamin C.

23

NANCY'S SCRAMBLER

4   eggs
1   tablespoon milk
Dash of Worcestershire sauce
2   drops hot sauce
¼   teaspoon salt
2   shakes of pepper
1   4-ounce can mushroom slices
1   tablespoon butter or margarine

Beat eggs in a mixing bowl with a beater or fork.

Add the milk, Worcestershire sauce, hot sauce, salt, and pepper, to eggs.

Drain the liquid from the mushrooms and spread them on a double layer of paper towels. Blot all the liquid from the mushrooms.

Melt butter slowly in a skillet. Add the mushrooms. Cook over a low heat, stirring constantly.

Add the egg mixture. Stir until eggs are firm but fluffy.

Serves 4.

GOLDEN PAVILION
PINEAPPLE HAM

1   ham slice ½-inch thick (center cut)
¾   cup orange juice
¼   cup brown sugar
6   pineapple slices

Heat a large skillet slowly (or heat an electric skillet to 350°).

Place the ham slice in the skillet. Cook for 10 minutes. Turn the slice over and cook 10 minutes more.

Remove ham from the skillet, but keep it warm. Pour orange juice into the skillet. Add brown sugar. Stir and cook until it boils.

Add the pineapple slices. Cook the ham on both sides in the juice mixture.

Place the ham on a serving platter. Put the pineapple slices on top of the ham and pour orange juice over the slices.

Serves 6.

NANCY'S TASTY TIP

For a touch of color, put a cherry in the center of each pineapple slice. To add a mystery taste, brush the ham with sauce from mustard pickles or horseradish mustard before pan-broiling it.

OLD STAGECOACH
SAUSAGE LOAF

2 *tablespoons butter or margarine*
2 *4-ounce cans mushroom pieces*
1 *egg*
2 *cups dry bread crumbs*
1 *pound fresh pork sausage*
1 *teaspoon paprika*

Heat the oven to 350°.

Melt the butter or margarine in a frying pan over low heat. Drain liquid from the mushrooms and add them. (If you wish to use fresh mushrooms, wash them first. Cut off stems, peel caps, and slice.) Cook slowly for 5 minutes. Stir often.

Break the egg into a bowl and beat. Add bread crumbs, sausage, and mushrooms to eggs. Mix well.

Form the mixture into the shape of a loaf. Place in small roasting pan. Sprinkle paprika over the loaf. Cover the pan. Bake for 30 minutes, remove the cover, and then bake 30 minutes longer.

Serves 4.

NANCY REVEALS

Paprika is a decoration which is also nutritious—it has vitamin C.

26

RIVER HEIGHTS FISH DISH

1   package frozen fish fillets
1   tablespoon cooking oil
Salt
Pepper
2   lemons
4   slices butter

Thaw the frozen fish fillets. Put the cooking oil in a baking pan. Lay the fish in the pan with the skin side down. Sprinkle on salt and pepper. Squeeze the juice of 1 lemon over the fish. Place a slice of butter on top of each fish fillet.

Heat the oven broiler.

Place the fish under the broiler for 8 minutes. Serve thin wedge of lemon with each fillet.

Serves 4.

A GOOD CATCH

Sprinkle fish with slivered, blanched almonds for the last 2 minutes of broiling. This will add more protein to your dish.

NED'S POTATO PANCAKES

3 or 4 large potatoes
1   egg
1   teaspoon salt
1   tablespoon flour
Cooking oil

Peel, wash, and dry the potatoes. Grate them until they measure 3 cups. Drain the water from them.

Break the egg into a bowl and beat it well. Add the potatoes, 1 tablespoon of cooking oil, salt, and flour to the egg. Mix together.

Heat just enough cooking oil to cover the bottom of the frying pan or griddle. Spoon 2 tablespoons of potato mixture into the hot frying pan for each pancake. Fry the pancakes until lightly browned on one side. Turn over and fry until lightly browned on the other side. Edges will be lacy when done.

This recipe is especially good served with applesauce.

Serves 2.

HANNAH'S CHEESE PUFFS

8   *slices white bread*
4   *slices sharp cheese*
2   *eggs*
2   *cups milk*
½   *teaspoon salt*
⅛   *teaspoon pepper*
¼   *teaspoon dry mustard*

Arrange 4 bread slices in the bottom of a large greased baking dish. Cover each with a slice of cheese. Place 4 more slices of bread on top of the cheese. Beat the eggs until they are frothy. Add the milk, salt, pepper, and dry mustard, mixing them well. Pour over the sandwiches.

Heat the oven to 350°.

Place the baking dish in the refrigerator and let it stand until the milk mixture is absorbed by the bread. Bake for 30 minutes. The sandwiches will be puffed and lightly brown when done.

Serves 4.

A TIDBIT

Use a cheddar cheese for this recipe. It is high in vitamin A and has the added advantage of melting easily.

RED GATE FARM TOMATOES

3   medium tomatoes
Salt
Pepper
Sugar
Butter
Parmesan cheese
Fine dry bread crumbs

Heat the oven broiler.

Wash the tomatoes, cut the stem ends and slice them in half. Sprinkle each half with salt, pepper, and sugar. Lay a small piece of butter on top of each.

Put the tomatoes, cut-side up, into a baking pan. Place in the broiler, 4 inches from the heat. Broil for 10 mintues.

Remove tomatoes from the broiler. Sprinkle each with Parmesan cheese and bread crumbs. Put the tomatoes back in the broiler for 3 more minutes.

Serves 6.

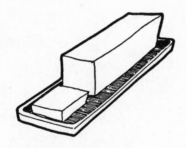

CAPTIVE BISCUITS

1   *3-ounce package cream cheese*
1   *stick butter*
1   *cup flour*

Let cream cheese and butter soften at room temperature, then mix them together. Add flour and stir well. Put mixture in refrigerator and let it chill overnight.

Then shape the dough into 8 small biscuits and put on baking sheet about 1 inch apart. Bake biscuits at 350° for 15 minutes. They will be browned when done.

CHAPTER 2

Time for Lunch

LILAC INN CONSOMMÉ

DETECTIVE BURGERS

OLD ALBUM MEATBALLS

TOGO DOGS

MYSTERIOUS LETTER CHILI

TOLLING BELL TUNA ROLLS

A KEENE SOUP

MUSKOKA SALMON SALAD

BURT'S PIZZA

SOUFFLÉ GRUEN

BUNGALOW MYSTERY SALAD

HIDDEN STAIRCASE BISCUITS

BESS'S SECRET CHOCOLATE WAFFLES

CARSON DREW'S CHEESECAKE

DANCING PUPPET PARFAIT

MAPLETON MILK SHAKE

LILAC INN CONSOMMÉ

2   carrots
2   small onions
½   cup chopped parsley
½   cup chopped celery
Salt
Pepper
2   cans beef or chicken consommé or bouillon

Wash and peel carrots. Cut off ends, then grate them into a bowl. Peel and grate the onions, adding them to the carrots.

Wash parsley. Cut off the stems. Dry on a paper towel. Snip the leaves with a clean scissors until you have chopped enough to make ½ cup and then add to the other vegetables.

Cut off the leaves of the celery and clean it before chopping. Stir it together with the carrots, onions, and parsley. Season with salt and pepper. Pour the consommé into a deep saucepan. Add the vegetables and bring the mixture to a boil. Turn the heat low and cook for 20 minutes. Serve piping hot.

Makes 4 portions.

A GRATE IDEA

To give the consommé a richer taste and more nutrition, sprinkle grated American cheese on top of each cupful. You'll be adding extra vitamin A to your dish.

DETECTIVE BURGERS

2   pounds ground beef
1   small onion
Salt
½   cup catsup
1   tablespoon mustard
1   tablespoon chili powder
24 slices bread or
12 hard rolls

Peel and chop the onion.

Sprinkle the ground beef with salt and mix in the onion. Place the beef and onion mixture in a skillet and cook over medium heat until brown. Add catsup, mustard, and chili powder and stir the ingredients together. Cover the skillet and turn the heat low. Cook for 30 minutes. Stir two or three times while cooking.

Lightly toast the bread slices or cut open the hard rolls and heat them. Spread the meat and vegetable mixture on the bread or rolls.

NANCY HAS A CLUE FOR YOU

Instead of plain bread, use English muffins, toasted potato bread, or garlic bread. (Be sure you serve parsley with the garlic bread. It's a great breath neutralizer!)

OLD ALBUM MEATBALLS

1½	pounds ground beef
½	cup uncooked rice
1	can tomato soup
1	tablespoon chopped onion
½	teaspoon pepper
1	teaspoon salt
½	soup can of water

Peel and chop a small onion; measure 1 tablespoon into a bowl. Add the ground beef, rice, salt, and pepper. Stir and shape the mixture into small balls.

Put the soup into a deep saucepan, add water and heat. When the soup mixture comes to a boil, carefully put in the meatballs. (Don't get splashed!) Cover the saucepan and turn the heat low. Cook for 1 hour.

Serves 6 people.

FOR VARIETY

Try using brown rice for this dish. It has more flavor and nutrition!

TOGO DOGS

¾   cup self-rising flour
¼   cup self-rising cornmeal
1   tablespoon sugar
1   teaspoon dry mustard
2   tablespoons dry onion soup
1   egg
½   cup milk
1   pound frankfurters (about 10)
10   wooden sticks
Corn oil

Mix flour, cornmeal, sugar, mustard, and onion soup together in a bowl.

Break the egg into another bowl, add the milk, and beat them together. Add it to the flour mixture and stir until the ingredients are well mixed.

Put a wooden stick into each frankfurter. Dry the franks with a paper towel and dust them with a little flour. Dip them into the batter so that each one is completely coated.

Heat a deep skillet half-filled with corn oil (375° for an electric skillet). Drop the frankfurters (sticks and all) into the hot oil. Fry them until they are brown. Take them out of the skillet and place them on paper towels to drain. Wipe the sticks dry.

DIP IN

Nancy puts bowls of catsup and mustard on the table to dip franks in.

37

MYSTERIOUS LETTER CHILI

2   medium onions
3   tablespoons cooking oil
2   #2 cans tomatoes
2   cans corned beef
3   1-pound cans kidney beans
1   tablespoon Worcestershire sauce
1½   teaspoons chili powder
Butter or margarine

Heat the oven to 350°.

Peel and chop the onions. Heat the cooking oil in a large skillet and cook the onion pieces slowly until brown. Drain liquid from the beans and combine them with the onion. Tear the corned beef into shreds and place it in the bean and onion mixture. Add tomatoes, Worcestershire sauce, and chili powder. Stir the mixture well.

Rub the sides and bottom of a baking dish with softened butter. Use a ladle to put the chili mixture into the greased dish. Bake for 30 minutes.

Serves 10-12.

NANCY'S DISCOVERY

By adding ¼ teaspoon of curry powder to the chili, a mysterious Far Eastern flavor is provided.

TOLLING BELL TUNA ROLLS

3   eggs
1   1-pound wedge American cheese
1   13½-ounce can tuna fish
2   tablespoons chopped onion
2   tablespoons pickle relish
¾   cup mayonnaise
6   hamburger buns

Put the eggs in a pan, cover them with water and bring to a boil. Cook slowly for 15 minutes. After letting them stand in cold water for a few minutes, peel the hard-boiled eggs. Chop into small pieces and cut the cheese into ¼-inch cubes. Place them in a bowl. Drain all liquid from the tuna fish and break the chunks into small pieces. Mix it with the eggs and cheese.

Add onion, relish, and mayonnaise to the mixture and stir.

Split the buns in halves and place the bottom halves in a shallow pan. Spread the mixture on them. Place the pan on the broiling rack and leave for 10 minutes. Remove them from the broiler. Then brown the inside of the top bun halves for ½ minute, and place them on top of the tuna mixture.

FOR A CHANGE

Nancy often replaces the tuna fish with a cup of cooked turkey or chicken—a good way to use those leftovers!

A KEENE SOUP

1 cup milk
4 level tablespoons peanut butter
¼ teaspoon celery salt
   or
¼ teaspoon cinnamon

Beat together the milk and peanut butter until thoroughly mixed. Add either celery salt or cinnamon. Place in saucepan over low heat, stirring and watching constantly. As it starts to boil, remove from heat and pour into pre-heated cups. Top with a teaspoon whipped cream. Sprinkle with paprika.

Makes 4 cups.

NANCY'S WARNING

Since this is a rich soup, she suggests only small quantities be served.

MUSKOKA SALMON SALAD

1   16-ounce can salmon
¼   cup peeled and chopped cucumber
2   tablespoons chopped onion
¼   cup heavy cream
¼   cup mayonnaise
1   teaspoon vinegar
Lettuce

Pull off the lettuce leaves, wash and dry them. Arrange them on 4 salad plates. Divide the salmon into 4 servings and place each serving on top of the lettuce leaves. Put the salad plates in the refrigerator to chill.

Mix together the mayonnaise, cream, chopped cucumber, onion, and vinegar. Pour the mixture on top of the salmon and lettuce when they are chilled.

This is a good summer luncheon dish.

NANCY'S NUTRITIONAL HINT

If you use spinach leaves instead of lettuce, you will be adding vitamin A and iron to your meal.

BURT'S PIZZA

6 English muffins
1 8-ounce can tomato sauce
Salt
Pepper
Oregano
½ pound grated mozzarella cheese

Split the English muffins into halves and cover each half with tomato sauce. Sprinkle with salt, pepper, and oregano seasoning. Cover with grated cheese. Broil the muffins until the cheese is melted and the tops are bubbly.
Makes 12 pizzas.

NANCY'S TASTY TOPPING

Put green olives or diced mushrooms on each pizza before covering it with cheese.

SOUFFLÉ GRUEN

4	*eggs*
2½	*cups milk*
2	*cups grated cheese*
1	*tablespoon butter*
¼	*teaspoon salt*
2	*shakes pepper*

Heat the oven to 375°.

Break eggs into a bowl and beat well. Add milk to the eggs. Beat the mixture while you slowly add the grated cheese. Add salt and pepper.

Cut the butter into small pieces and stir it into the mixture.

Rub the bottom and sides of a glass baking dish with softened butter. Pour the cheese mixture in the greased baking dish.

Bake for 25 minutes.

Serves 4-6.

BUNGALOW MYSTERY SALAD

2   6¾-ounce cans frozen orange juice
2   lemons
1   6-ounce can pineapple juice
2   yellow or red bananas
1   cup ginger ale
1   cup sugar
24 paper muffin cups

Squeeze the lemons and put the juice through a strainer. Thaw frozen orange juice in a bowl. Add the strained lemon juice and the pineapple juice. Mash bananas and add them to the mixture. Pour in the ginger ale and sugar. Stir well.

Put paper muffin cups in the muffin pans. Ladle mixture into the cups. Place salads in the freezer and leave until frozen.

AN EXTRA TOUCH

For topping, stir some crushed pineapple and chopped dates into whipped cream cheese. You will get protein from the cheese and dates and vitamin C from the pineapple.

HIDDEN STAIRCASE BISCUITS

1 can 10-count refrigerator buttermilk biscuits
2 tablespoons butter
10 sugar lumps
¼ cup maraschino cherry juice

Heat the oven to 425°.

Line a baking pan with aluminum foil. Separate biscuits and place them on the pan. Melt the butter in a small saucepan. Spoon or brush the tops of the biscuits with melted butter.

Dip each sugar lump into the cherry juice. Push the lumps into the tops of the biscuits.

Bake the biscuits for 10 minutes.

Serve piping hot.

A MYSTERY TASTE

Try using maple sugar, which is much sweeter than regular white sugar. But use smaller lumps.

45

BESS'S SECRET
CHOCOLATE WAFFLES

2	squares unsweetened chocolate
1	stick (4 ounces) butter
1	scant cup sugar
2	eggs
½	teaspoon salt
1 ½	cups flour
½	teaspoon cinnamon
¼	teaspoon almond extract
1	teaspoon vanilla flavoring

Let the butter stand at room temperature until it is soft. Mix the butter and sugar together. Melt and cool the chocolate and mix it with the butter and sugar.

Add the eggs, salt, flour, cinnamon, almond extract, and vanilla flavoring to the chocolate mixture. Stir until well blended.

Heat the waffle iron. Spoon in the batter and heat until waffles are brown.

Makes 4-6 waffles.

NANCY SUGGESTS

Put a scoop of vanilla ice cream on top of each waffle. Sprinkle cinnamon or nutmeg over it.

CARSON DREW'S CHEESECAKE

2 *8-ounce packages cream cheese*
⅔ *cup sugar*
3 *eggs*
¼ *teaspoon almond extract*

Heat the oven to 350°. Let the cream cheese stand at room temperature until it is soft. Gradually add sugar to the cream cheese and mix thoroughly.

Break eggs into the cream cheese mixture one at a time. Stir each time you add an egg. Pour in the almond extract and stir well. Put the mixture into a springform pan. Bake for 50 minutes.

Cool it!

Serves 4-6.

DOUBLE DELIGHT

Make your cheesecake even more delicious with a crumb crust.

2 *cups fine graham-cracker crumbs*
½ *cup sugar*
½ *cup melted butter or margarine*

Mix crumbs and sugar in a bowl. Add melted butter and mix well.

Press onto sides and bottom of an 8-inch springform pan. Chill in refrigerator before adding the filling.

DANCING PUPPET PARFAIT

1   cup apricot nectar
27 large marshmallows
1   cup heavy whipping cream

Bring the apricot nectar to a boil, then remove it from the heat. Cut each marshmallow into 4 pieces and place them in the hot syrup. Stir until the marshmallows melt. Let the mixture cool.

Put the cream into a bowl and beat until stiff. After the marshmallow mixture cools, mix it with whipped cream, stirring lightly. Spoon the mixture into 6 parfait glasses or sherbet cups and put them in the refrigerator for at least 4 hours before serving.

TO BE DIFFERENT

You can substitute plain yogurt for the cream. Just stir it into the cooled marshmallow mixture. It is lower in calories and higher in protein.

MAPLETON MILK SHAKE

1   pint vanilla ice cream
1   quart cold milk
½   cup maple syrup

Let the ice cream soften and put it in a mixing bowl with the milk and maple syrup. Beat it with an electric or hand mixer. Pour it into glasses and serve ice cold. Makes 12 half-cup servings.

Be daring and try different flavors of ice cream (chocolate is good) to mix with the maple syrup. Nancy turns this delicious milk drink into a surprise float when she puts a scoop of ice cream into each glass.

FOR A HIDDEN NUTRITIOUS TREAT

Try this same recipe using ½ cup of black-strap molasses in place of the maple syrup.

Kitchen Mystery

Late one afternoon Nancy was hurriedly called to the home of Mrs. Russo, a neighbor, to help her find a valuable heirloom ring. The piece was strangely missing just before she was to give it to her niece at a birthday dinner party. No one else had been in the house all day. Mrs. Russo, who had selected the ring from her jewel box that morning, was positive she had not worn it in the kitchen while preparing dinner.

Nancy, however, refused to overlook a single possibility. After Mrs. Russo had gone upstairs to dress, Nancy began a search. She figured that if the woman had unknowingly dropped the ring into some food she was preparing, it would have sunk to the bottom. First Nancy examined the aspic salad, then the cream of mushroom soup. No ring! Next she looked at the blueberry muffins, still in their twelve-cup pan.

"If the ring's in a muffin," she thought, "it would have been spooned up last, so the jewelry would be in one of the end cups."

Nancy began to break open the muffins. No luck on one, two, three. Then she halved the fourth.

The next moment she cried out, and raced up the stairs. "Mrs. Russo, the ring was in a muffin! Your gift is safe!" As the woman thanked Nancy profusely, the girl added with a smile, "How about my whipping up another batch of muffins for your party?"

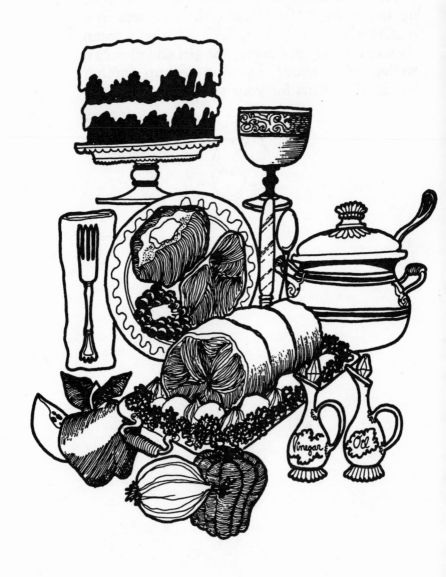

CHAPTER 3

Time for Dinner

SLEUTH SOUP

CODED STEAK ROLLS

THE CASE OF THE SMOTHERED
PORK CHOPS

RINGMASTER'S SECRET CHICKEN

IVORY CHARM SHRIMP CURRY

DAVE'S DEVILED POTATOES

CASSEROLE TREASURE

MYSTERY CORN PUDDING

THE COUSINS' SPECIAL
CAULIFLOWER

DOUBLE JINX SALAD

CROOKED BANISTER CORN BREAD

MRS. MARVIN'S MAGIC MUFFINS

FIRE DRAGON SPICED FRUIT

TWISTED CANDLES PEACH CRISP

OLD CLOCK ICE CREAM PIE

INVISIBLE INTRUDER'S
COCONUT CUSTARD

TEA LEAF MESSAGE

LEMONADE DISGUISE

SLEUTH SOUP

1   *can beef consommé or bouillon*
1   *consommé can tomato juice*
½   *cup heavy whipping cream*
Parsley flakes

Combine the consommé and tomato juice in a saucepan and warm over low heat.

Pour cream into a bowl and whip.

Pour soup into cups, and put a spoonful of whipped cream on top of each.

Sprinkle parsley flakes over the cream.

Makes 6 soup cups.

CODED STEAK ROLLS

1   round steak ¼-inch thick (approximately
        2 pounds)
6   bacon strips
1   medium onion
Salt
Pepper
Flour
1   tablespoon butter or margarine
¼   cup hot water
Toothpicks

Cut steak into 6 individual pieces. Sprinkle each piece with salt and pepper. Top with bacon strips.

Peel and cut an onion into thin slices and put several on each steak. Roll up the meat pieces and fasten them with toothpicks. Lightly coat each steak roll with flour.

Melt butter in a skillet over low heat. Fry the steak rolls until they are brown on both sides. Add the hot water. Cover the skillet over a low heat for 30 minutes. Check the steak rolls several times while they are cooking and add more water if the meat begins to stick to the skillet.

A HOT TIP

To make the steak "hotter," spread a little mustard sauce on the meat before rolling it up.

THE CASE OF THE SMOTHERED PORK CHOPS

4   thick pork chops
½   cup uncooked rice
1   medium onion
1   lemon
1   can beef consommé or bouillon
Salt
Pepper

Heat the oven to 325°.

Cut fat off the pork chops. Slowly melt the fat in a skillet over low heat. Put the chops in and brown on both sides. Pour rice into a baking dish and place the browned chops over the rice.

Peel and cut the onion into 4 slices and place 1 on each chop. Sprinkle with salt and pepper. Cut the lemon into 4 slices and set on top of the onion slices. Pour the consommé over the chops. Cover the dish. Bake for 1 hour.

A GOOD SUBSTITUTE

Change the flavor of this dish by substituting a can of mushroom soup plus ½ can of water for the consommé.

RINGMASTER'S SECRET CHICKEN

4	chicken breasts
1	cup sour cream
1	tablespoon Worcestershire sauce
½	teaspoon red hot sauce
⅛	teaspoon garlic salt
1½	teaspoons paprika
1	teaspoon salt
1	cup fine dry bread crumbs

Wash the chicken and dry with paper towels. Mix together sour cream, Worcestershire sauce, hot sauce, garlic salt, paprika, and salt. Place the chicken breasts in this mixture and leave in the refrigerator overnight to marinate.

Take the chicken out of the mixture and roll each breast in the bread crumbs. Put them in a large baking dish, arranging them in a single layer. Cover the dish and place in the refrigerator for at least 1½ hours.

Heat the oven to 325°. Uncover the dish and bake the chicken for 1 hour and 15 minutes.

EXPERIMENT

Make your own bread crumbs: crush stale bread or crackers with your fingers, then sift them until you have a cup of fine crumbs.

IVORY CHARM SHRIMP CURRY

2   cups cooked rice
1   10-ounce package frozen cooked shrimp
1   can frozen condensed cream of shrimp soup
1   cup sour cream
1   large onion
1   tablespoon butter or margarine
½   teaspoon curry powder
Paprika
Parsley flakes

Heat the oven to 375°.

Thaw shrimp as directed on the package. Spread cooked rice in the bottom of a baking dish.

Chop an onion into small pieces. Melt butter in a skillet. Cook the onion over low heat until tender but not brown. Stir in the soup until smooth. Add sour cream and curry powder until ingredients are blended. Put in the shrimp.

Pour this mixture over the rice. Sprinkle it with paprika and parsley flakes. Bake for 20 minutes.

Serves 4.

FOREIGN FLAVOR

For Far Eastern intrigue, serve small bowls of crushed salted peanuts, chopped hard-boiled eggs, and chutney for guests to sprinkle over the shrimp dish.

DAVE'S DEVILED POTATOES

4-6 medium potatoes
1   teaspoon salt
3   tablespoons softened butter
⅓ cup warm milk
    (or, in place of the above ingredients, one
    envelope of instant potatoes)
½ cup sour cream
1   tablespoon mustard
1   tablespoon sugar
2   tablespoons chopped green onions

Wash, pare, and cut potatoes into 4 pieces each for faster cooking. Cover with boiling water, add salt, and cook (covered) from 20 to 40 minutes until tender when tested with a fork. Drain. Add softened butter and warm milk. Mash until free of lumps. (If you are using instant potatoes, follow directions on package.)

Heat the sour cream in a small saucepan over a low flame. Add mustard and sugar to the sour cream and mix until well blended. Stir potatoes into the sour cream mixture. Blend in chopped onion. Put the potato mixture into a 1-quart casserole.

Heat the oven to 350°. Bake for 12 minutes.
Serves 4.

cont'd

NANCY'S TOPPER

Add a surprise by frying 4 slices of bacon in the skillet over low heat until crisp. Drain on paper towels, crumble, and sprinkle on top of deviled potatoes.

CASSEROLE TREASURE

2   packages frozen French-style string beans
      or
2   cans string beans
1   can cream of mushroom soup, not diluted
½   cup slivered almonds or
1   3¾-ounce package slivered almonds
½   teaspoon Worcestershire sauce
½   pound sharp cheese, grated

Heat the oven to 350°. If you are using frozen beans, cook according to the package directions and drain. Add mushroom soup, almonds, and Worcestershire sauce. Mix well.

Pour the mixture into a greased casserole. Top with grated cheese. Bake for ½ hour or until cheese is melted and beans are piping hot.

Serves 6.

A SHARP CHOICE

For the topping choose a sharp cheddar cheese because it melts easily and contains a lot of vitamin A. If you like, mix bread crumbs with the grated cheese.

MYSTERY CORN PUDDING

3   eggs
1   16-ounce can creamed corn
¾   cup milk
1   tablespoon Worcestershire sauce
1   tablespoon sugar
1   tablespoon flour
1   tablespoon minced onion
1   tablespoon chopped parsley
6   cheese-flavored crackers

Heat the oven to 325°.
Break the eggs into a bowl and beat well. Mix in corn, milk, Worcestershire sauce, and sugar. Add flour, onion, and parsley, and stir until well blended.
Grease a medium-sized casserole dish. Pour in the corn mixture. Crumble crackers and spread them on top. Bake for 1 hour.
Serves 4.

FROM ONE AMATEUR TO ANOTHER

Want to vary the taste? Into the mixture stir pieces of chopped tuna fish. Serve with a hot cheese sauce made of 1 cup milk, 2 table-spoons butter, 2 tablespoons flour, 1 cup grated cheese, all blended together over low heat.

THE COUSINS'
SPECIAL CAULIFLOWER

1   cauliflower
4   eggs
3   small onions
1   teaspoon flour
1   teaspoon salt
½   teaspoon pepper
Cooking oil

Wash the cauliflower and separate into flowerettes. Put them in a saucepan and cover with water. Bring them to a boil and cook for 15 minutes. Then drain the water and chop each flowerette into very small pieces.

Break eggs in a bowl and beat. Peel onions and chop into small pieces. Mix cauliflower, onion, flour, salt, and pepper with eggs. Shape into balls.

Fill a deep-fat fryer or skillet with cooking oil and heat until hot. Drop cauliflower mixture, a ball at a time from a spoon, into hot oil. Fry until golden brown.

Makes 25 cauliflower balls.

FLAVOR AID

Serve a hot cheese sauce over them. See Nancy's variation on Mystery Corn Pudding.

DOUBLE JINX SALAD

4 peeled Bartlett pear halves (fresh or canned)
1 teaspoon mayonnaise
1 cup cottage cheese
Green food coloring
Crisp lettuce leaves
2 green olives

Mix together mayonnaise, several drops of food coloring, and cottage cheese. Fill the center of each pear half with this mixture. Put the pear halves together to form whole pears; the cheese mixture should hold the halves in place.

Stand pears upright on lettuce leaves. Place green olive on top of each pear.

Serves 2.

A CRISP RESCUE

To keep lettuce leaves crisp and full of nutrition, peel off as many as you need from the head. Rinse them off and pat dry with paper towels. Put leaves in a plastic bag and chill in the refrigerator.

CROOKED BANISTER
CORN BREAD

2	cups yellow corn meal
1	cup flour
1	teaspoon salt
4	teaspoons baking powder
1	large or 2 small eggs
1⅓	cups milk
2	tablespoons butter or margarine
1	tablespoon sugar

Heat the oven to 400°.

Blend corn meal, flour, salt, baking powder, and sugar, and put them into a sifter or shaker.

Beat eggs. Add milk to them and stir. Slowly sift the dry mixture into the eggs and milk, and stir. Melt butter and slowly add to the batter.

Grease a square 8-inch pan or a muffin tin. Pour in the batter, spreading evenly. Bake 15 minutes for muffins and 18 minutes for corn bread. Cut the bread into squares.

Makes 12 servings.

TASTY ACCENT

Serve the bread or muffins with healthful blackstrap molasses. It gives corn bread a delicious taste when it is spread on like jam.

MRS. MARVIN'S MAGIC MUFFINS

1   *cup self-rising flour*
3   *tablespoons mayonnaise*
½ *cup milk*

Heat the oven to 400°.
Mix the flour and mayonnaise in a mixing bowl. Add milk, a small amount at a time, stirring only until dry particles are moistened. Grease a 6-muffin tin and spoon in the mixture. Bake for 20 minutes.

NANCY SUGGESTS

If you don't have self-rising flour, add 1½ teaspoons of baking powder to 1 cup of regular flour.

FIRE DRAGON SPICED FRUIT

2	cups peach halves
2	cups pear halves
1	small jar maraschino cherries
2½	cups pineapple chunks
⅓	cup butter or margarine
¾	cup brown sugar
1	teaspoon curry powder

Heat the oven to 325°.

Drain peaches, pears, cherries, and pineapple. Dry them on paper towels. Arrange the fruit in a 2-quart casserole, mixing the pieces.

Melt butter in a skillet over low heat. Add brown sugar and curry powder and stir until smooth. Pour over the fruit.

Bake, uncovered, for 1 hour.

Serve with meat or as a salad.

NANCY'S HELPFUL TIP

This fruit dish becomes even tastier if it is left covered in the refrigerator overnight. Before serving, reheat it for 20 minutes at 350°.

TWISTED CANDLES
PEACH CRISP

1   *stick (4 ounces) butter*
2   *16-ounce cans sliced peaches*
1   *cup light brown sugar*
1   *cup flour*
1½   *teaspoons cinnamon*

Heat the oven to 375°.

Let butter soften outside the refrigerator. Drain peaches and dry them on paper towels.

Mix sugar, flour, and cinnamon in a bowl. Put the softened butter into this mixture. Combine ingredients with a fork until well mixed into a dough.

Place peaches in the bottom of the baking dish. Spread the dough over them. Bake on the bottom shelf of the oven for 50 minutes.

Makes 6 servings.

DETECTIVE DYNAMITE

For an extra delicious taste, add a scoop of ice cream to each serving. This recipe can even be used as a birthday cake. Insert a tiny candle in each portion and light before serving.

67

OLD CLOCK ICE CREAM PIE

1   quart vanilla ice cream
½   cup frozen strawberries or raspberries
24   cream-filled chocolate cookies

Let the ice cream and frozen berries soften and mix them together.

Heat the oven to 350°.

Mash cookies with a rolling pin or crush them in a blender until very fine. Grease a pie plate and line with the crumbs. Bake this pie shell for 8 minutes. Take it out of the oven, let it cool, and fill with the ice cream mixture. Put into the freezer and chill thoroughly.

NANCY'S IDEA

On the pie form the face of a clock with chocolate jimmies or chocolate bits. Set the "hands" at the hour you plan to serve the dessert.

INVISIBLE INTRUDER'S
COCONUT CUSTARD

1	stick (4 ounces) butter
4	eggs
1½	cups sugar
½	cup self-rising flour
2	cups milk
1	teaspoon vanilla flavoring
1	7-ounce package flaked coconut

Heat the oven to 350°.

Melt the butter. Break eggs into a bowl, beat and add sugar, flour, milk, melted butter, vanilla, and coconut. Stir well.

Grease a baking dish and pour in the mixture. Bake 50 minutes.

Serves 6-8.

NANCY'S SECRET INGREDIENT

To add nutrition and a mysterious taste, stir about 1 tablespoon of pineapple juice into the coconut flakes before adding them to the mixture.

TEA LEAF MESSAGE

4   tea bags
2   cups sugar
Juice of 4 lemons
3   sprays fresh mint leaves, crushed

Put 4 quarts of water into a large saucepan. Bring to a boil, turn off the heat, and add the tea bags. Steep tea until it is a strong, dark color.

While tea is still warm, add sugar, lemon juice, some lemon rind, and crushed mint. Let it stand for several hours, then remove the tea bags.

Put plenty of ice in a large pitcher and pour the tea over it.

A MESSAGE FROM NANCY

Before tossing out the tea bags, spread the leaves on a platter. See if you can find a "message" in them. Two, three, or four leaves together might represent the number of people you will join at a party.

70

LEMONADE DISGUISE

2   cups cranberry juice
3¼   cups water
5 or 6 whole cloves
1   stick cinnamon
⅓   cup sugar
1   6-ounce can frozen concentrated
         lemonade, softened

Mix cloves, cinnamon, cranberry juice, and water in saucepan. Place over medium heat and bring to a rolling boil. Cover. Remove from heat and let stand for 5 minutes.

Place strainer over large pitcher and pour in the liquid. The strainer will catch the spices which you can discard. Add sugar and stir until dissolved. Add lemonade and mix well. Reheat. When the liquid is hot, but not boiling, pour into cups.

Serves 8.

SLEUTH DISCOVERY

Nancy finds that half an orange slice and a sprig of mint or a green cherry for every cupful makes a pretty decoration and a tasty one, too!

CHAPTER 4

Picnic and Patio Get-Togethers

MIRROR BAY TRIPLE DECKER
LARKSPUR LANE SANDWICHES
BLACK KEY MYSTERY PATTIES
LEANING CHIMNEY CONES
CROSSWORD CIPHER CHICKEN
SHADOW RANCH BARBECUED BEANS
EMERSON COOKOUT POTATOES
THE DREWS' ONION SPECIAL
DIARY CHICKEN SALAD
MOONSTONE CASTLE CARROT SALAD
MISS HANSON'S DEVILED EGGS
WOODEN LADY WALNUT TIDBITS
WHISTLING BAGPIPES CRUNCHIES
WHISPERING STATUE SHERBET
SCARLET SLIPPER RASPBERRY PUNCH
IMPOSTOR TEA

MIRROR BAY TRIPLE DECKER

For each sandwich:
3   slices toast
1   thin slice boiled ham
1   slice cooked turkey or chicken breast
1   large or 2 small slices tomato
1 or 2 tablespoons coleslaw
Mayonnaise
Salt
Pepper

To make coleslaw, shred cabbage into a bowl. Add a little salt and pepper and enough mayonnaise to make it moist.

Peel and slice tomatoes. Bring the ham, turkey, and slaw to room temperature. Toast bread, butter 2 slices, and spread mayonnaise thinly on the third.

Lay turkey on the mayonnaise slice. Add tomato and a sprinkle of salt. Cover the turkey with the dry side of 1 slice of buttered toast. Add ham and top it with coleslaw. Cover the third slice of buttered toast, butter-side down.

AN ALIAS

In place of ham and turkey, use tuna fish and slices of mild cheese.

LARKSPUR LANE SANDWICHES

Butter or margarine
1 loaf sliced white sandwich bread
¼ cup crystallized (or preserved) ginger
¾ cup orange marmalade

Let butter or margarine soften outside the re-frigerator. Cut the crusts off bread slices, then butter one side of each. Mix the ginger and marmalade. Spread a thin layer of ginger mixture on the buttered side of half the number of slices. Top them with the remaining buttered bread slices.

NANCY'S VARIATION

For a mysterious tart taste, substitute lemon marmalade for orange.

BLACK KEY MYSTERY PATTIES

2 pounds ground beef
2 teaspoons salt
½ teaspoon pepper
¼ cup sliced stuffed green olives
¼ cup sliced celery stalks
1 cup whole cranberry sauce
1 teaspoon lemon juice
1 teaspoon chopped onions

Sprinkle salt and pepper over ground beef and mix them into the meat. Shape into 8 patties.

Place the patties on outdoor grill about 3 inches above glowing coals. Grill for 15 minutes. Turn the patties and cook for 5 minutes on the other side.

Cut olives into thin slices. Mix them with the celery, cranberry sauce, lemon juice, and chopped onion.

Heat this mixture on the stove or a corner of the grill while cooking patties. Pour this mixture over patties to serve.

NANCY SUGGESTS

If you prefer a tart sauce, use catsup, Worcestershire, or A-1 sauce, instead of the cranberry sauce.

LEANING CHIMNEY CONES

12 slices bologna
6 sprigs parsley
2 pimentos
4 cups radishes
¼ cup finely cut chives
1 pint cottage cheese
Salt
Pepper

Remove the rind from the bologna. Place separate slices on a tray.

Wash parsley. Cut off stems. Dry on a paper towel. Cut leaves finely with clean scissors. Chop pimentos into small pieces.

Cut off the root end of radishes and scrub well. Chop into small bits.

Combine parsley, pimentos, radishes, and chives in a bowl. Add cottage cheese and stir well. Place a spoonful of this mixture on each slice of bologna.

Sprinkle with salt and pepper. Roll each slice into the shape of a cone. Hold the cones together with toothpicks. Serve cones so they stand up in a large bowl.

A NUTRITIONAL DECORATION

Insert a sprig of parsley into the top of each cone. Parsley is colorful and full of vitamin C.

CROSSWORD CIPHER CHICKEN

3 cups unsweetened cracker crumbs, rolled very fine
2 teaspoons garlic salt
4 tablespoons parsley flakes
3 tablespoons Parmesan cheese
2 sticks (8 ounces) margarine
1 2½ pound fryer, cut into serving pieces

Heat the oven to 375°. Place crackers between 2 pieces of wax paper. Crush with a rolling pin until very fine. Put 3 cups of crumbs into a bowl. Add garlic salt, parsley flakes, and Parmesan cheese. Mix well.

Melt margarine in a saucepan over low heat. Dip each piece of chicken into it, then roll in the crumb mixture.

Cover a cookie sheet with foil and put the chicken pieces on the sheet. Bake for 1 hour. Serves 6.

A SAUCY SOLUTION

Serve the chicken with a sauce made of 1 cup chicken gravy and 1 cup milk seasoned with salt and pepper and thickened slightly with 1 tablespoon flour. Dissolve the flour in ⅛ cup water before adding to the boiling gravy.

cont'd

GRILLING TIME

If you want to barbecue the chicken on an outdoor grill, omit the cracker crumbs. Cook the pieces six inches above the hot coals. Turn and baste with melted margarine every twenty minutes.

SHADOW RANCH
BARBECUED BEANS

2   10-ounce cans pork and beans
1   large onion
2   sticks (8 ounces) margarine
1   tablespoon dry mustard
¼   cup sugar
¾   cup dark brown sugar
¼   cup catsup
1   tablespoon Worcestershire sauce
Salt
Pepper

Heat the oven to 300°.
Peel the onion, and chop into small pieces. Melt margarine in a saucepan over very low heat. Grease bottom and sides of a baking dish.
Put onion pieces, melted margarine, pork and beans, dry mustard, sugar, brown sugar,

cont'd

79

catsup, and Worcestershire sauce in the baking dish and mix well. Sprinkle this mixture with salt and pepper. Cover the dish. Bake for 2 hours.

Serve with applesauce, hot or cold.

Makes 8 portions.

EMERSON COOKOUT POTATOES

5 *slices bacon*
3 *large-sized potatoes*
Salt
Pepper
1 *large onion*
½ *pound cheddar cheese*
1 *stick (4 ounces) butter or margarine*

Fry bacon in a skillet over low heat until crisp. Drain on paper towels. Crumble bacon into small pieces.

Peel potatoes, slice them thin, then put them on a large piece of foil. Sprinkle with salt and pepper. Spread bacon crumbs over potatoes. Peel the onion, cut thin slices, and place them on the crumbs.

Cut cheese into small cubes and dot over onion slices. Cut butter into squares and cover the cheese with them. Wrap the foil around this potato mixture and seal the edges tightly. Cook over hot coals for 1 hour. Turn over several times while cooking.

Serves 4.

cont'd

NUTRITIOUS AND DELICIOUS
Cheddar cheese is a good source of vitamin A which provides healthy skin and hair.

THE DREWS' ONION SPECIAL

6 *medium-sized onions*
6 *beef bouillon cubes*
3 *teaspoons butter*
Salt
Pepper

Peel onions. Scoop out a small hole in the top of each onion. Put a bouillon cube and ½ teaspoon butter in the hole of each onion. Sprinkle with salt and pepper.

Wrap each onion in a piece of foil, sealing tightly. Put onions on hot coals on outdoor grill and cook for 45 minutes. Turn over several times while cooking. Unwrap onions with two forks and serve while piping hot.

GOOD GO-TOGETHERS
Use as a vegetable with meat or poultry and serve with sprigs of parsley for decoration.

DIARY CHICKEN SALAD

2   cans mandarin orange or tangerine sections
¼   cup white, seedless grapes
¼   cup salted almonds
1   banana
2   cups cooked chicken, cut into small cubes
½   cup mayonnaise
18 canned pineapple rings

Drain orange sections. Dry on paper towels. Wash grapes and cut them in half. Chop almonds into small pieces. Peel the banana and slice into thin round pieces.

Combine orange sections, grape halves, chopped almonds, banana slices, and chicken cubes in a bowl. Add mayonnaise and mix well.

Put 3 pineapple rings on each guest's plate, forming a triangle. Pile the chicken salad on top of the pineapple rings.

Serves 6.

A TANGY TWIST

Cut $^1 2$ pound sharp cheddar cheese into small cubes. Mix with the fruit and chicken. (You may have to add extra mayonnaise.)

MOONSTONE CASTLE
CARROT SALAD

2 1-pound cans diced carrots
1 medium onion
1 can tomato soup
3/4 cup sugar
3/4 cup vinegar
1/2 cup salad oil
1 teaspoon salt
1 teaspoon pepper
1 teaspoon paprika
1 tablespoon dry mustard

Drain carrots. Peel the onion and cut into thin slices. Separate the slices into rings. Line the bottom of a casserole dish with diced carrots. Cover them with a layer of onion rings. Alternate layers of carrots and onion rings until all are used.

In a separate bowl mix soup, sugar, vinegar, oil, salt, pepper, paprika, and dry mustard. Beat for 3 minutes.

Pour the mixture over the carrots and onion rings. Cover the dish and put in the refrigerator for 24 hours.

Serves 8.

A YUMMY COMBINATION

Try serving this with barbecued spare ribs.

MISS HANSON'S DEVILED EGGS

6   eggs
¼ cup mayonnaise
1   teaspoon prepared mustard
1   teaspoon vinegar
⅛ teaspoon salt
Dash of pepper
Paprika

Place the eggs in a saucepan. Cover with cold water. Boil for 15 minutes. Remove from heat and drain off hot water. Let eggs stand in cold water a few minutes, then peel and cut them lengthwise in half. Scoop out the yolks and mash them in a bowl. Add mayonnaise, mustard, vinegar, salt, and pepper, and mix thoroughly.

Spoon the mixture back into the hollows of the egg whites. Sprinkle paprika on top of each egg half.

A GOOD TOPPER

Decorate each egg with a slice of olive.

WOODEN LADY
WALNUT TIDBITS

Roquefort cheese
Sweet dairy butter
Walnut halves

Let butter soften out of refrigerator. Crumble Roquefort cheese. (Base the amount of Roquefort cheese and butter you use on the number of tidbits you plan to serve.)

Measure equal parts of crumbled Roquefort cheese and softened butter. Mash the cheese and butter together. Spread a small amount of cheese mixture on a walnut half and cover with the other half.

Put the tiny walnut tidbits in the refrigerator to chill before serving.

A FUN SUGGESTION

Experiment with this recipe for tasty surprises. Spread the cheese mixture between other tiny foods such as cherry tomato halves, cucumber slices, or party rye bread slices.

WHISTLING BAGPIPES CRUNCHIES

1   6-ounce package butterscotch morsels
½   cup peanut butter
1   3-ounce can chow mein noodles
1   cup miniature marshmallows

Put butterscotch morsels and peanut butter into a 1-quart saucepan. Melt together by cooking them over very low heat for 5 minutes. Then take butterscotch mixture off the stove. Add the noodles and marshmallows and stir together.

Cover the bottom of a baking pan with wax paper. Lay 1 teaspoonful of mixture at a time on the wax paper. Shape them into strips resembling bagpipes and put them in groups. Let this candy stand until firm.

Makes about 35 crunchy bagpipes.

GIVEAWAY IDEA

These candies make nice gifts, too!

WHISPERING STATUE SHERBET

6 8-ounce orange drinks
1 8¹₄-ounce can crushed pineapple
1 14-ounce can condensed milk
1 6-ounce can concentrated orange juice

In a pitcher mix together the orange drinks, pineapple, condensed milk and orange juice. Remove the dividers from empty ice trays.

Pour the mixture into the trays and put in refrigerator. To prevent the mixture from separating, stir at 10-minute intervals until freezing begins.

TRY IT!

Nancy likes to serve this on ice cream cones, or as a combination with vanilla ice cream.

SCARLET SLIPPER
RASPBERRY PUNCH

1   3-ounce package raspberry gelatin
1   package raspberry drink powder mix
1   6-ounce can frozen lemonade concentrate
1   cup sugar
3   quarts water
Ice

Mix gelatin as directed on the package in a 1-gallon container. Add the drink powder mix to the gelatin.

Stir in lemonade concentrate. Add sugar and stir until the sugar dissolves. Add water and keep stirring. Fill the rest of container with ice.

Makes 4 quarts of punch.

TART TOUCH

Before you serve the punch, add the rind of fresh lemons. Grate or use a knife to cut off tiny pieces of the rind which contains vitamin D.

IMPOSTOR TEA

1 quart apple juice
8 cloves
2 sticks cinnamon
1 quart orange juice
1 quart pineapple juice
Cheesecloth bag

Pour apple juice into a large saucepan. Put cloves and cinnamon in the cheesecloth bag and place in the pan with the juice. Simmer for 20-25 minutes. Remove the cheesecloth bag from the pan. Add the orange and pineapple juices. Sweeten to your taste.

Keep the "tea" hot, but under the boiling point. Or chill and serve in punch cups.

Makes about 12 servings.

NANCY SAYS

Use this for a "tea" party with sandwiches or cookies.

CHAPTER 5

Nancy Shares Her Holiday Secrets

Nancy has suggested complete holiday dinners
in this chapter. She had given directions for the
particular recipes she enjoys preparing.

NEW YEAR'S DAY
MRS. FAYNE'S FAMOUS RICE

VALENTINE'S DAY
BROKEN LOCKET MERINGUES

WASHINGTON'S BIRTHDAY
GEORGE'S CHERRY COBBLER

ST. PATRICK'S DAY
**MOSS-COVERED MANSION FRUIT
GELATIN**

HAUNTED BRIDGE LOG

APRIL FOOL'S DAY
? ? ? ? ?

EASTER
SPIDER SAPPHIRE SPICED CHERRIES

JEWEL BOX EASTER EGGS

MOTHER'S DAY
MYSTERIOUS MANNEQUIN
CASSEROLE

FATHER'S DAY
ATTORNEY SHRIMP SAUCE

CHOCOLATE RIDDLE

END OF SCHOOL
AUNT ELOISE'S GRADED COLESLAW

FOURTH OF JULY
OLD ATTIC STUFFED TOMATO

FLAG CAKE SYMBOL

HALLOWEEN
WITCH TREE APPLES

GHOSTLY POPCORN

THANKSGIVING
EFFIE'S PUMPKIN SOUP
CRANBERRY SURPRISE

CHRISTMAS
PINE HILL PUNCH
HIDDEN WINDOW DESSERT

NEW YEAR'S EVE
**MRS. NICKERSON'S HOLIDAY
COOKIES**

NEW YEAR'S DAY

Fruit Cup or Juice

Lamb (leg, rolled shoulder or chops)

MRS. FAYNE'S FAMOUS RICE

Peas (fresh, frozen or canned). If you are a Southerner, you will want black-eyed peas for good luck!

Soft Rolls

Apple Butter

Iceberg Lettuce with your favorite dressing

Hot Plum Pudding or Gingerbread with hard sauce or whipped cream

94

MRS. FAYNE'S FAMOUS RICE

1   cup raw rice
5   tablespoons butter or margarine
3½   cups chicken broth
3   medium onions
1   sweet red or green pepper

Melt 2 tablespoons butter in a saucepan. Put in the rice and heat until golden. Add 1 cup chicken broth. Bring to a boil, then lower the heat. Cover and cook for 15 minutes or until the liquid has been absorbed. Add the rest of the chicken broth and cook covered until this liquid has been absorbed.

Peel and chop onions. Wash and dice pepper. Melt 3 tablespoons butter in another small pan. Cook the onions and pepper until golden and glossy. Combine with cooked hot rice and serve.

Makes 4 servings.

DIFFERENT TASTE

Try using a cup of cooked brown rice. Prepare it well in advance, since it takes about 2 hours to cook.

VALENTINE'S DAY

Onion Soup (Sprinkle paprika on top of each portion. Serve grated cheese with it.)

Veal Roast, cutlet or chops with cheese or tomato sauce
Shell Macaroni or Mashed Potatoes
Hearts of Lettuce (Cut cold beet slices into heart shape and place around salad.)
Broccoli with Hollandaise Sauce (Use leftover egg yolks from MERINGUES recipe to make sauce.)

Warm Rolls

BROKEN LOCKET MERINGUES

BROKEN LOCKET MERINGUES

1	large package frozen strawberries
6	eggs
1 ¼	teaspoon salt
1 ½	teaspoon cream of tartar
1	cup sugar
½	pint heavy whipping cream

Heat the oven to 250°.

Take strawberries from the freezer and thaw. Break each egg open and separate the white part from the yellow yolk. Put all the egg whites in a mixing bowl. (You will not use the egg yolks in this recipe.)

When egg whites reach room temperature, add salt and cream of tartar. Beat this mixture until almost stiff. Slowly stir in ¾ cup of sugar. Beat until all is dissolved.

Line a greased baking pan with heavy brown paper upon which you have outlined 4-6 hearts. Spoon some batter onto each heart and mold it into the shape of the heart. Leave the sides higher than the center so that you have heart-shaped shells. Bake for 1 hour. Let stand in a turned-off oven (door closed) at least 10 minutes.

Chop the thawed strawberries into tiny pieces and set aside.

Pour the cream into a mixing bowl. Beat, slowly adding ¼ cup sugar. Continue beating

cont'd

until the cream is stiff enough to stand in peaks.

Take the shells from the oven. When cool, fill the center of each with chopped strawberries. Cover with whipped cream.

DON'T WASTE!

Use at least two of the unused egg yolks in your hollandaise sauce with the broccoli.

WASHINGTON'S BIRTHDAY

Tomato, Vegetable, or Cranberry Juice

Baked Pork Chops
Baked Potato (Serve with butter, margarine or sour cream)
Hot Applesauce
Creamed Spinach

Soft Rolls

GEORGE'S CHERRY COBBLER

GEORGE'S CHERRY COBBLER

6   tablespoons butter
1   cup prepared biscuit mix
¾   cup sugar
1   cup milk
¼   teaspoon cinnamon
1   21-ounce can cherry pie filling

Heat the oven to 350°. Place the butter in a casserole dish and put it in the oven to melt.

Combine the biscuit mix, sugar, milk, cinnamon, and cherry filling. Pour these ingredients into a casserole with melted butter. Bake for 45 minutes or until the crust is golden. Serve warm with whipped cream or ice cream.

Serves 6.

YOU CAN SPREAD THIS AROUND!

Toast ½ cup wheat germ in the oven for a few minutes and sprinkle over the whipped cream on each serving.

ST. PATRICK'S DAY

Split Pea Soup

Corned Beef
Boiled Cabbage or Cauliflower
Parsley Potatoes

Irish Soda Bread

Mustard or Horseradish Sauce

MOSS-COVERED MANSION FRUIT
GELATIN
HAUNTED BRIDGE LOG

MOSS-COVERED MANSION
FRUIT GELATIN .

2   packages lime gelatin
2   cups boiling water
1   30-ounce can mixed fruits
10 ounces crushed pineapple

Melt gelatin in boiling water. Add juice from the fruit, plus enough cold water to make 2 cups liquid. Then put in the fruit. Stir well. Pour into a greased mold, a bowl, or custard cups. Place in the refrigerator and let stiffen.

To loosen gelatin from mold, set it in hot water for only a few seconds. Serve plain or with mayonnaise or other salad dressings.

A GOOD CHOICE!

If you wish to serve this as a dessert, prepare this topping: ¼ cup heavy cream, ¼ cup honey, and ¼ cup lemon juice, all mixed well. Pour over each serving.

HAUNTED BRIDGE LOG

1   *package chocolate wafers (special round type for icebox cake)*
1   *pint heavy whipping cream*
2   *tablespoons sugar*
2   *teaspoons vanilla flavoring*
Green food coloring

Whip cream until it forms peaks. Fold in sugar, vanilla, and a few drops of green food coloring.

Stack 3 or 4 wafers together at a time, putting a teaspoonful of green whipped cream between each one. Save one wafer for later. Place the stack sideways on a dish to form a log. Cover the log with the rest of the cream.

Crumble the wafer you have saved and sprinkle on top. Refrigerate for at least 3 hours. Cut diagonally at a 45° angle.

Serves 10.

A MINT HINT

Add a teaspoon of mint extract to the cream while whipping.

APRIL FOOL'S DAY

EASTER

Honeydew Melon Slice or Grapefruit Half

Baked Ham
SPIDER SAPPHIRE SPICED CHERRIES
Scalloped Potatoes
Buttered Wax Beans

Biscuits

Vanilla Ice Cream with Butterscotch Sauce

JEWEL BOX EASTER EGGS

SPIDER SAPPHIRE
SPICED CHERRIES

1   *quart black Bing cherries*
½   *cup vinegar*
3   *cups sugar*
½   *teaspoon cloves*
½   *teaspoon allspice*

Wash and pit the cherries. Combine with vinegar, sugar, cloves, and allspice in a large pan. Cook over low heat for several hours. When the syrup is thick, the cherry relish is ready.

JEWEL BOX EASTER EGGS

2   *sticks (8 ounces) butter*
1   *8-ounce package cream cheese*
3   *1-pound boxes confectioners' sugar*
8   *ounces semisweet chocolate*
1   *tablespoon butter*
1   *2-inch square paraffin*
¼   *teaspoon vanilla flavoring*

Let butter and cream cheese come to room temperature. Put them in a large bowl and mix them together. Slowly add the sugar until well blended. Shape this mixture into small eggs

cont'd

105

about the size of a teaspoon. Store in refrigerator for at least an hour.

Put water in the bottom of a double boiler and bring to a boil. Place chocolate, 1 tablespoon butter, paraffin, and vanilla flavoring in the top of the double boiler. Let this mixture melt over the boiling water, stirring well. Dip each chilled egg into the mixture. Put coated eggs back in the refrigerator for at least 15 minutes.

Make about 100 delicious small Easter eggs.

FOR GOODNESS SAKE!

Put nutritious surprises in the eggs. Chop up 4 ounces seedless raisins and 2 ounces unblanched almonds and add them to the butter and cream cheese mixture.

MOTHER'S DAY

Pineapple Juice

MYSTERIOUS MANNEQUIN
CASSEROLE

Asparagus (fresh or frozen) served with melted butter, cream sauce, or Hollandaise Sauce

Ice Cream

Brownies or Cookies

106

MYSTERIOUS MANNEQUIN
CASSEROLE

Cooking oil
1   medium onion
1   green pepper
1   3- or 4-ounce can sliced or chopped
    mushrooms
1   pound ground round beef or chuck
2   cups shell macaroni
3   8-ounce cans tomato sauce
1   12-ounce can creamed-style corn
1   pound sharp cheese, grated

Heat the oven to 300°.

Start with a big skillet! Wash pepper and remove seeds, stem and white membrane. Peel onion and chop it with green pepper. Fry in a small amount of oil until glossy. Then brown meat in these ingredients.

Drain mushrooms and add to the mixture. Remove from heat.

Boil the macaroni until tender. Drain and add to the meat.

Add the tomato sauce and creamed corn and mix well.

Grease a casserole dish and put in the mixture. Sprinkle grated cheese on top. Bake for an hour.

Serves 6-8.

FATHER'S DAY

Shrimp Cocktail
ATTORNEY SHRIMP SAUCE

Steak
Tossed Salad with Roquefort Dressing
French Fries
Onion Rings

CHOCOLATE RIDDLE

ATTORNEY SHRIMP SAUCE

1   *cup catsup*
1   *cup mayonnaise*
10 *drops Tabasco sauce*
4   *teaspoons grated onion*
1   *clove garlic, finely grated*
Crisp lettuce leaves

Combine all ingredients in a mixing bowl. Stir well. Spoon the mixture over very cold shrimp served on crisp lettuce leaves in glass cups or small saucers. Makes 2 cups.

CHOCOLATE RIDDLE

5   *large eggs*
1   *cup very fine sugar*
3   *tablespoons cocoa*
½ *pint heavy whipping cream*
½ *teaspoon vanilla flavoring*
1   *heaping teaspoon sugar*

Break eggs, putting the yolks in one mixing bowl and the whites in another. Beat the whites with a hand or electric beater until they form peaks. Set aside. Beat the yolks, gradually adding sugar and cocoa. When well mixed, fold into the whites. Heat the oven to 350°.

Grease a cookie sheet, or a 12 x 20 x ½ inch pan. Line with wax paper and grease the paper. Spread the mixture on it. Bake for 20 minutes.

cont'd

109

Turn the cake onto a clean dish towel and remove the wax paper. Cover with a clean, moist dish towel until thoroughly cooled. Whip the cream, adding 1 teaspoon vanilla flavoring and a heaping teaspoon sugar. Beat until the cream forms peaks. Spread cream on the cake. Roll the cake into the shape of a jellyroll, then roll it in the towel. Refrigerate.

When ready to serve, remove the towel and put the cake on a platter or a decorative wooden board. Cut into ¾-inch slices.

DELICIOUS FIND

Sprinkle chocolate jimmies over the cream just before you roll up the cake.

END OF SCHOOL OUTDOOR PARTY

Franks in a Blanket (Hot Dog in a Roll!)
Relishes—Catsup, Pickle Relish, Mustard
Potato Chips with Cheese Dip
AUNT ELOISE'S GRADED COLESLAW

Ice Cream Cones

AUNT ELOISE'S
GRADED COLESLAW

1   medium-sized cabbage head
3   carrots
¾   cup small raisins (or dried currants)
Mayonnaise

Wash and grate the cabbage and carrots. Mix. Add enough mayonnaise to moisten. Put in a large quantity of small raisins or dried currants and stir well.

Be ingenious and mold the coleslaw in the shape of something having to do with your school program, hobby, social activity, etc.

A SOUR SUGGESTION

To make this dish somewhat tart, leave out the raisins or currants, and add ¼ cup diced sweet pickles and 1 tablespoon pickle juice.

111

FOURTH OF JULY

OLD ATTIC STUFFED TOMATO
Vegetable Salad (lettuce, celery, carrots,
cucumber, radish)
Corn on the Cob

FLAG CAKE SYMBOL

OLD ATTIC STUFFED TOMATO

¼ *pound sausage meat*
4 *firm tomatoes*
½ *cup bread crumbs*
2 *tablespoons consommé or bouillon*
1 *small onion, minced*
1 *clove garlic, minced*
2 *tablespoons chopped parsley*
Butter or margarine

Heat the oven to 300°.

Slice tops off the tomatoes. Scoop out the centers. Discard seeds and chop up the centers. Set aside the tops and centers.

Moisten bread crumbs with consommé.

Cook minced onion and garlic in butter until soft.

Mix together with sausage meat, bread crumbs, onion, garlic, tomato centers, and parsley.

Stuff tomatoes with this mixture and sprinkle with fine bread crumbs. Dot with butter and put on the tomato caps. Bake in a lightly oiled baking dish for 35 minutes.

FLAG CAKE SYMBOL

1 *package white cake mix*
1 *box confectioners' sugar*
2 *tablespoons warm cream or milk*
1 *teaspoon vanilla flavoring*
Pinch of salt
Cocoa
Blueberries
Raspberries

Bake the cake, following the instructions on the package, in a pan 9 x 13 x 2. Let cool. Make a white icing by combining the confectioners' sugar with the warm cream or milk, the vanilla flavoring, and the salt. Beat well. Then frost

cont'd

the cake. Decorate the top with a "flag picture." Use cocoa for the pole, blueberries for the stars, and raspberries for the red stripes.

COME CLEAN!

If you use fresh berries, wash them by letting them soak in cold water for 5-10 minutes. Then put them in a strainer and gently run more cold water over them.

HALLOWEEN

WITCH TREE APPLES

GHOSTLY POPCORN

WITCH TREE APPLES

2 cups maple-blended syrup
1 cup sugar
¹₄ teaspoon cream of tartar
9 wooden skewers or sticks
9 medium apples
1 cup peanuts

   Insert a wooden skewer into the stem of each
apple. Crush peanuts by placing them between two pieces of wax paper, and rolling a
rolling pin across the paper.
   Heat water in the bottom of a double boiler
until it bubbles. Put the syrup in the top part
of the boiler and bring to a boil. Add sugar and
cream of tartar, stirring until sugar is dissolved. Cover and boil for 3 minutes. Uncover
and cook the mixture over a medium-high heat
until it reaches 300° on a candy thermometer,
or until a tiny amount dripping off a spoon
spins a hard and brittle thread.
   Remove the double boiler from the stove. Dip
each apple into the candy mixture, turning it to
coat evenly. Swirl the bottom half of each
apple in crushed peanuts. Press the peanuts
lightly to the apple with your hand so that they
will stick to the candy.
   Grease a large piece of aluminum foil with
butter. Put the apples (peanut ends down) on
the foil to cool.

cont'd

FOR AN EXTRA TREAT

Mix leftover peanuts into the candy mixture. Spread on the greased aluminum foil. Let the candy cool. Break into pieces, like brittle, for a yummy snack.

GHOSTLY POPCORN

2   cups sugar
½ cup corn syrup
½ cup water
2   5½-ounce packages popped popcorn
25 small flat wooden sticks

Put the sugar, corn syrup, and water in a saucepan. Cook over low heat until it reaches 245° on a candy thermometer, or until a spoonful of mixture dropped into cold water forms a hard ball.

Pour the cooked syrup over popcorn and stir with a spoon to mix it well. Mold the popcorn into balls around the ends of wooden sticks. Work quickly to finish molding the popcorn before the syrup becomes hard!

NANCY LETS YOU IN ON A SECRET

You can also use this recipe for Christmas. Mold the popcorn into balls without the wooden sticks. When they are hard, wrap them in cellophane paper and hang them on the Christmas tree.

THANKSGIVING

EFFIE'S PUMPKIN SOUP

Roast Turkey with Dressing (or Chicken or
Duck)
Mashed Potatoes
Candied Sweet Potatoes
Creamed Onions
Mashed Turnips
CRANBERRY SURPRISE
Olives
Celery

Pumpkin or Apple Pie

Bowl of Fresh Fruit

Nuts

Mints

EFFIE'S PUMPKIN SOUP

1   cup cooked rice or
3   tablespoons raw rice, boiled
¾   cup half-and-half cream
¹₂ cup canned pumpkin
2   cups canned chicken broth
2   teaspoons lemon juice
2   tablespoons sugar

Cook the rice as directed on the package, then place in the refrigerator. When chilled, put the rice in a blender with ½ cup of half-and-half. Blend at low speed until the mixture is smooth. Add the rest of the half-and-half (¼ cup), pumpkin, chicken broth, lemon juice, and sugar. Mix these ingredients with a beater until well blended.

Put the soup into the refrigerator for at least an hour. Serve chilled.

Makes 4 soup cups.

NANCY WARNS

If you do not have a blender, use an egg-beater and whip slowly. Beating too fast and too long will turn the cream into butter!

CRANBERRY SURPRISE

1 *pound fresh cranberries*
2 *oranges*
²⁄₃ *cup sugar*
2 *packages raspberry gelatin*
4 *ounces blanched almonds, chopped*

Wash and drain cranberries. Cook in ½ cup of water until they burst.

Grate orange skins, then cut orange slices into small pieces. Add the grated orange peel, the orange sections, and the juice to the cranberries.

Dissolve gelatin in 1½ cups of boiling water. Add sugar, gelatin, and chopped almonds to the cranberry-orange mixture. If it is too thick, add ½ cup of water and put in a greased gelatin mold. Set in refrigerator until stiff.

When serving, decorate with cucumber rings or parsley.

Serves 8.

A SUGGESTION FROM NANCY

Make individual portions by using custard cups or a muffin pan instead of a mold, and serve as a salad on lettuce leaves, with or without dressing.

CHRISTMAS

PINE HILL PUNCH

Roast Beef (in its own juice as gravy)
Roast Potatoes
String Beans (fresh, frozen or canned)
Glazed Carrots

Celery
Olives
Radishes
Pickles

HIDDEN WINDOW DESSERT

Fruit Cake

PINE HILL PUNCH

6   cups apple cider
1   cinnamon stick
¼   teaspoon nutmeg
¼   cup honey
2   tablespoons lemon juice
3   teaspoons grated lemon rind
1   20-ounce can unsweetened pineapple juice

Put the apple cider and cinnamon stick into a large saucepan and bring to a boil. Lower the heat, cover, and cook for 5 minutes.

Stir in nutmeg, honey, lemon juice, lemon rind, and pineapple juice. Cook over low heat, without a cover, for 5 more minutes. Serve hot or cold in punch cups to wish your friends a happy holiday.

Fills 20 cups.

A HONEY OF AN IDEA!

Try to buy uncooked raw honey. It's more nutritious!

HIDDEN WINDOW DESSERT

1   package cherry gelatin
1   package orange gelatin
1   package lime gelatin
1   package lemon gelatin
1   cup pineapple juice
¼   cup sugar
1½   tablespoons melted butter
12   graham crackers, crushed
4   cups whipped cream or other whipped
       topping

In a saucepan boil enough water to make 1 cup. This means you must start with a little more than a cup. Dissolve the cherry gelatin in this. Stir well. Add ½ cup cold water and pour the gelatin into an ice tray with no divider.

Do the same with the orange and lime gelatin separately. (Use the same pan, but rinse it each time.) In the same pan again, boil the pineapple juice with sugar. Dissolve the lemon gelatin in this. Add ½ cup cold water. Let set in a large mixing bowl to the syrupy stage. Fold in the whipped cream.

When firm, cut the cherry, orange, and lime gelatins into cubes. Fold them into the lemon gelatin mixture. Grease a springform pan. Stir melted butter into the crushed graham crumbs and spread on the bottom of the pan. Pour in the mixture. Chill for 12 hours. You'll have many colored windows in each slice of cake!

A CHEERY CHANGE

For a different flavor, substitute cubes of mint jelly for the lime gelatin cubes.

NEW YEAR'S EVE

(Midnight Snack)

Tiny Minced Ham Sandwiches
Tiny Minced Chicken Sandwiches
Eggnog

MRS. NICKERSON'S HOLIDAY COOKIES

Fresh Fruit

MRS. NICKERSON'S
HOLIDAY COOKIES

1   stick (4 ounces) butter
2   eggs
1   cup sugar
1   tablespoon milk
½   teaspoon vanilla flavoring
½   teaspoon salt
1   teaspoon baking powder
1½   cups flour
2   squares bitter chocolate, melted   or
2   tablespoons cocoa

You need 3 mixing bowls! Mix butter, sugar, salt, baking powder, and flour together in one of the bowls. In another bowl, beat the eggs and stir in the milk and vanilla. Add slowly to the dry mixture and stir.

Place ¼ of the batter in the third bowl. Add the melted chocolate or cocoa. Heat the oven to 350°.

Grease a cookie sheet. Drop both kinds of batter on it, a teaspoon at a time. Flatten together with a wet fork. Add white, red, or green sugar as decoration. Bake for 12 minutes. Remove from the sheet while warm.

Makes 50 cookies.

A DREW CLUE

To keep cookies fresh in a jar, put half an apple in with them.

CHAPTER 6

Album of International Recipes

HONG KONG FORTUNE COOKIES
NEAR EAST FRUIT KABOBS
ENGLISH POPOVERS
FRENCH QUICHE
VERSAILLES AU CHOCOLAT
GERMAN KALBSROULADEN
GREEK BAKLAVA
INDIA BHAPA DOI
ITALIAN SALSA DI POMIDORO
MEXICAN STEW
OLD MEXICO'S GUACAMOLE SALAD
POLYNESIAN PUNCH
ENGLISH STYLE CHOPS WITH HERBS
CHINESE SHRIMP CAKES
WEST INDIES SALAD

HONG KONG FORTUNE COOKIES

¾ cup butter or margarine
2 cups sugar
1 teaspoon vanilla flavoring
3 eggs
1 cup sifted flour
60 intriguing fortunes written on small strips of
   paper

Let butter soften outside the refrigerator.

In a mixing bowl put sugar and butter and blend together until fluffy. Add vanilla. Then add eggs to the mixture, one at a time. Beat well after adding each egg. Then add flour and beat thoroughly.

Heat the oven to 375°.

Grease the cookie sheets, then dust lightly with flour. Drop rounded teaspoons of dough at least 2 inches apart on each sheet.

Bake for 20 minutes and remove. With a wide spatula, loosen each cookie from the sheet. Place a folded fortune on each cookie. Gently fold the cookies in half with the fortune inside. Pinch edges together, then twist in the centers.

Makes 60 fortune cookies.

NANCY SHARES A SECRET

While putting a fortune inside each cookie, keep the sheet warm. This will make cookies easier to work with.

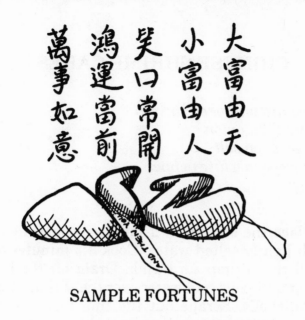

SAMPLE FORTUNES

You will have a pleasant surprise soon.

You will make a delightful new friendship in the next few weeks.

A happy cook makes a happy friend.

You will find good fortune soon.

You will be baking for someone special in the near future.

Keep a smile on your face and you will always keep a friend.

Happiness will find you if you let it.

You will take a fun trip soon!

If you save your money, you will be rewarded with a nifty surprise.

Note: Have fun composing some yourself.

CHINESE SHRIMP CAKES

1 pound uncooked shrimp
¹₂ medium onion
²₃ teaspoon salt
¹₈ teaspoon white pepper
1 egg

Place the shrimp in a large saucepan filled with lightly salted water. Cook 3-5 minutes or until the shrimp turn pink. Drain off the hot water and pour cool water over the shrimp. Remove shells. Scrape out the thin black veins with a knife and wash each shrimp.

Chop the shrimp, peel the onion, and chop it into very small pieces. Mix them together with salt and pepper. Beat an egg and add to the shrimp mixture. Stir well.

Put ¹₂-inch of cooking oil in a skillet. Heat the oil until hot. Drop 1 tablespoon at a time of the shrimp mixture into hot oil. Cook shrimp cakes until golden brown on each side. Drain grease from each shrimp cake on paper towels.

If desired, pour on sweet and sour sauce or apricot marmalade.

Serves 4.

NANCY SUGGESTS

Buy precooked shrimp, fresh or frozen, and start with paragraph two of this recipe.

ENGLISH POPOVERS

2 *eggs*
1 *cup milk*
1 *cup all-purpose flour*
½ *teaspoon salt*

Break the eggs into a bowl. Add milk, flour, and salt. Stir well until only small doughy lumps remain in the batter.

Grease the bottom and sides of cup sections of an iron muffin pan or custard cups. Use a plastic pitcher or measuring cup to fill each cup ⅓ to ½ full of batter.

Put popovers in a cold oven. Turn the heat to 450°. Bake for 30 minutes.

Makes 8 large or 12 small popovers.

WARNING

If you use plain flour, add ½ teaspoon of baking powder. If you use custard cups, place them on a cookie sheet.

ENGLISH STYLE
CHOPS WITH HERBS

12 lamb chops, 1 inch thick
2 teaspoons dried basil
2 teaspoons marjoram
2 teaspoons thyme
2 teaspoons salt

Wipe each lamb chop with a damp paper towel or cloth.

In a bowl mix together the herbs—basil, marjoram, thyme, and salt. Rub the herb mixture on both sides of each chop. Put in a covered bowl. Place in the refrigerator for an hour.

Heat the oven broiler. Place the chops under the broiler 4 inches from the heat. For medium-rare chops, broil 6 minutes on one side, 4 minutes on the other. For well-done chops, cook 5 minutes longer.

Serves 6 hungry people 2 each!

FRENCH QUICHE

1   frozen pie crust
3   tablespoons cooked crisp bacon
1   cup Swiss cheese, grated or crumbled
1   cup light cream
3   eggs
Salt
White pepper
½ teaspoon nutmeg
Dash of cayenne pepper

Thaw the pie crust. Heat the oven to 350°. Sprinkle bacon bits over the crust, and spread grated cheese on top of the bacon.

Put cream, eggs, salt, pepper, nutmeg, and cayenne pepper into a blender, or use an egg-beater. Mix well. Pour the mixture into the pie crust. Bake the pie for 30 minutes. It will be golden brown when done. Cut into wedges, like a regular pie, and serve hot.

Serves 6 people.

VERSAILLES AU CHOCOLAT

1   4-ounce bar sweet chocolate
1   tablespoon sugar
½ cup cream
2   egg yolks
½ teaspoon vanilla flavoring

Heat water in the bottom of a double boiler. Put chocolate in the top part and set in the bottom part. Let chocolate melt. Slowly stir in the sugar until smooth. Remove the top of the double boiler from heat.

Break open the eggs and separate the whites from the yellow yolks. (You will not use the egg whites.) Put the egg yolks in a bowl. Add vanilla flavoring and beat. Slowly pour hot chocolate into the egg mixture, stirring briskly Transfer into very small cups or containers. Put into the refrigerator to chill.

Before serving them, Nancy decorates each cup with a spoonful of whipped cream, topped by a cherry.

A SAVING TIP

Covered in the refrigerator, egg whites will keep for 10 days.

GERMAN KALBSROULADEN
(Rolled Veal Scallopini)

8 *thin-sliced veal cutlets*
2 *uncooked slices bacon*
½ *cup beef stock or bouillon (add more if desired)*
1 *small dill pickle*
1 *small onion*
Flour
Salt
Pepper
Toothpicks

Lay veal slices on a flat surface. Salt and pepper lightly. Dice bacon, pickle, then peel and chop the onion. Spread the mixture over the meat. Roll slices and fasten with toothpicks.

Dust the rolled-up meat with flour and brown in butter, margarine, or oil in a skillet. Add beef stock. Cover and simmer over low heat for about 45 minutes.

Serves 4.

FOR MORE NUTRITION

Add ½ tablespoon wheat germ to ½ cup of flour before you dust it on the veal.

GREEK BAKLAVA

12 *frozen patty shells, thawed*
3   *cups finely chopped walnuts or pecans*
1   *cup honey*

Heat water slowly in the bottom of a double boiler. Put honey in the top of the double boiler and keep it warm till you use it.

Line an 8 x 8 x 2-inch pan with foil, folding it over the rim of the pan. Grease lightly and set aside.

Lightly flour a dough board (or table top). With a smooth, clean rolling pin, flatten out 1 thawed patty shell. Place a second thawed shell on top and flatten into the first. Put the third patty shell on top of these.

Roll out until you have a 9-inch square of dough. This will make a thin flaky crust. With a sharp knife trim it down to an 8½-inch square. Carefully place this 8½-inch layer evenly in the bottom of the 8-inch pan, pressing the extra ½-inch of pastry along the sides.

Heat the oven to 425°.

Sprinkle layer with 1 cup chopped nuts and ¼ cup warm honey. Make 3 more thin layers of pastry from the shells, as directed above. Cover with same amounts of filling. Use the last layer as topping. Bake for 20-25 minutes. Let cool slightly. Brush the top with the last of the warm honey (¼ cup).

Remove from pan by lifting up the foil and peeling it away. Cut the baklava into 12 squares. Serve with more honey or with whipped cream.

WATCH OUT!

Baklava is a very rich, sweet dessert. Serve it in very small portions.

INDIA BHAPA DOI

2 *12-ounce cans evaporated milk*
1 *8-ounce carton plain or flavored yogurt*
¾ *cup sugar*
½ *teaspoon ground cardamon, nutmeg, or cinnamon*
Unsalted almonds, pecans, or other nuts and raisins

Heat the oven to 350°.
Beat the yogurt, evaporated milk, and sugar for 2-3 minutes in a bowl. Pour into the casserole dish. Bake uncovered for 30-35 minutes.
Remove from the oven. Sprinkle ground cardamon (or cinnamon or nutmeg) on top. Then sprinkle generously with almonds (or other nuts) and raisins. Put in the refrigerator for 2-3 hours.
Serves 4-6.

ITALIAN SALSA DI POMIDORO
(Tomato Sauce)

2   tablespoons olive oil
1   medium onion
1   16-ounce can tomatoes
1   6-ounce can water
1   6-ounce can tomato paste
2   teaspoons sugar
1   teaspoon oregano
½   teaspoon salt
Freshly ground pepper

Heat olive oil slowly in a large saucepan. Peel and chop the onion. Cook it in the oil until soft, but not brown.

Cut up the tomatoes. Combine with paste,

sugar, oregano, salt, and a bit of pepper. Pour into the saucepan. Stir well. Cover and simmer over low heat for 45 mintues.

Serve over spaghetti and sprinkle with Parmesan cheese.

Serves 4.

With the spaghetti, serve Italian bread: spread butter and garlic powder on the bread and warm in the oven.

NANCY SUGGESTS

When cooking spaghetti, add a teaspoon of oil so the strands will not stick together

MEXICAN STEW

1 *pound ground round beef or chuck*
1 *15-ounce can kidney beans*
1 *can tomato soup*
1 *soup can water*
1 *teaspoon chili powder*
Cooking oil

Cover the bottom of a skillet with cooking oil. Crumble the meat into it. Cook over medium heat until brown. Add beans, soup, water, and chili powder. Stir well. Heat the mixture until it boils, then lower temperature. Cover the skillet and cook slowly for 30 minutes.

Serves 4.

cont'd

Give a taste of intrigue to this recipe by adding ½ cup chopped onion and ½ cup diced green pepper at the same time you add the beans, soup, water, and chili powder.

OLD MEXICO'S GUACAMOLE SALAD

2 *large ripe avocados*
1 *ripe tomato*
2 *tablespoons finely chopped onion*
1 *teaspoon lemon juice*

Peel the avocados and dice into small pieces. Peel the tomato and dice it. With a fork, mash the avocado and tomato pieces together to make a paste. Add the onion and lemon juice. Mash again. Put the salad in the refrigerator to chill.

To make lettuce-leaf cups for salad, cut out the core of the head. Peel off as many lettuce leaves as you need. Rinse them off thoroughly. Serve the dish with your favorite dressing.

Makes 4 servings.

A HEALTH HINT

Try this low-calorie dressing: in a cup of plain yogurt put 1 teaspoon honey and 1 teaspoon lemon. Mix well.

POLYNESIAN PUNCH

2   cups papaya concentrate
2   cups apricot nectar
2   cups orange juice
½   cup lemon juice
1   cup sugar
2   quarts ginger ale
1   17-ounce can fruit cocktail

In a large pitcher combine papaya concentrate, apricot nectar, orange juice, lemon juice, and sugar. Stir the mixture well. Let stand for 1 hour to blend the flavors.

When ready to serve, pour the mixture into a punch bowl. Add the ginger ale. Float a ring or block of ice in the punch bowl. Drain the fruit cocktail and stir it into the punch.

Makes enough to fill 25 punch cups.

cont'd

SPECIAL EFFECT

Go tropical—float fresh flowers on top of the punch. For a change, scoop out a large fresh pineapple and serve the punch from the empty skin. Use the scooped-out pineapple pieces either in the punch or as an appetizer or dessert. You'll have to fill the pineapple skin more than once!

NEAR EAST FRUIT KABOBS

2 apples
1 can mandarin oranges
12 apricot halves (canned)
12 dried prunes
6 green figs (canned)
1 cup orange marmalade
½ cup orange juice
6 kabob sticks or skewers

Wash and core the apples. Cut each into 6 wedges. Drain juice from the mandarin oranges, canned apricot halves, and canned figs. On a kabob stick place a mandarin orange slice, then an apple wedge, an apricot half, a dried prune, a fig, another dried prune, an apricot half, an apple wedge, and finally a mandarin orange slice.

Mix the orange marmalade and orange juice together. Brush the fruit with this mixture, coating each piece well. Fill 5 other sticks the same way. Cook these fruit kabobs under a

broiler for 5 minutes. Serve piping hot.
Serves 6 people.

WEST INDIES SALAD

1   pound cooked fresh lump crab meat
1   medium onion
4   ounces salad oil
3   ounces vinegar
Salt
Pepper

Peel the onion and chop into very small pieces. Put half the amount in a bowl. Place crab meat lumps on top of the chopped onion. Spread the rest of the chopped onion over the crab meat. Flavor with salt and pepper.

Pour oil, then vinegar, then 4 ounces ice water over the mixture. Cover the bowl and put in the refrigerator for 12 hours.

To make lettuce-leaf cups for salad, cut out the core of the head. Peel off as many lettuce leaves as you need. Rinse them off thoroughly. Toss the mixture lightly before serving in the crisp lettuce cups.

Makes 4 portions.

A HINT FROM NANCY

Want to add a mysterious crunch? Cut $^2_3$ *cup celery into very small pieces and mix with the onion.*

CHAPTER 7

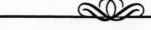

Diary of Giveaway Treats

BRASS BOUND TRUNK CANDY
MISSING MAP CHEESE WAFERS
HAUNTED SHOWBOAT PRALINES
THE CORNINGS' CARAMEL COOKIES
VELVET MASK BALL
WINNING TOASTED NIBBLES
TOMMY'S FRUIT YUMMIES
APPLE BUTTER REWARD
VANISHING NUT BREAD

BRASS BOUND TRUNK CANDY

16 ounces semisweet chocolate pieces
⅔ cup sweetened condensed milk
1 teaspoon vanilla flavoring
⅛ teaspoon salt
¾ cup dry oatmeal
⅓ cup any kind chopped nuts, unsalted (less
    than a 3-ounce package)
¼ cup flaked coconut

Put water in the bottom of a double boiler and bring to a slow boil. In the top of the boiler melt chocolate pieces. Then add condensed milk, vanilla, salt, oatmeal, chopped nuts, and coconut to the melted chocolate. Stir until well blended.

Grease the bottom and sides of an 8-inch-square pan. Spread the candy mixture in the greased pan. Put in the refrigerator to chill.

When the candy is firm, cut into squares. Wrap each candy square individually in cellophane or plastic wrap. Fill a glass vase or metal canister with the candy for a delicious holiday gift.

NANCY'S HOLIDAY HINT

If you are making the squares for Valentine's Day, decorate the container with paper hearts for an appropriate touch.

146

MISSING MAP CHEESE WAFERS

1   pound sharp cheddar cheese
7   tablespoons butter
1   cup flour
½   teaspoon salt
¼   teaspoon red pepper
1   cup pecans or other nuts

Grate the cheese and put it into a mixing bowl. Add butter, flour, salt, and pepper. Mix together and work into a well-blended dough.

Chop pecans into small pieces. Add them to the cheese dough. Mix well. Lift the dough onto a sheet of wax paper or dish. Shape the dough into a roll.

Keep in the refrigerator overnight. When you are ready to bake, slice the dough into thin circles. Place the circles on a greased cookie sheet. Heat the oven to 325° and bake for 10 minutes. For a change, try currants or small raisins in place of the nuts.

A HOLIDAY SPECIALTY

Cut off the front panel of a Christmas or other holiday card with an attractive scene and glue it to the cover of a plain box. Fill the box with the golden crisp cheese wafers. To prevent breakage, put a little round sheet of wax paper between every 2 wafers.

HAUNTED SHOWBOAT
PRALINES

1 cup white sugar
1 cup brown sugar
½ cup water
¼ cup butter
1 teaspoon vinegar
1 pound pecan halves

Put the white and brown sugar, water, and butter in a saucepan. Cook over low heat, stirring often, until a drop placed in cold water forms a soft ball. Add the vinegar and cook for 1 minute longer.

Using a paper towel, rub the cooking oil over a large sheet of wax paper. Drop a tablespoon of candy mixture on an oiled surface to make each praline. Quickly press several pecan halves into each candy piece before it gets cold. Pralines should be about 3 inches in diameter and rather thin.

Add a mysterious taste by putting a mixture of pecans and walnuts in each piece.

PRETTY PLAN

Wrap several pralines in a candy box or in a piece of colored cellophane or tissue paper. Tie a thick strand of colored yarn around the package for a festive-looking gift.

THE CORNINGS'S
CARAMEL COOKIES

3   cups sugar
12   tablespoons butter
1   6-ounce can evaporated milk
1   4-ounce package instant butterscotch
      pudding mix
3½   cups quick-cooking oats

Place the sugar, butter, and evaporated milk in a large saucepan. Bring the mixture to a boil, stirring several times.

Take the saucepan off the heat. Add the pudding and oats. Stir well. Let the mixture cool for 15 minutes.

Line a tray with wax paper. Drop the cookie mixture on the wax paper a teaspoon at a time. Cookies will become firm when completely cooled.

A NOVEL IDEA

For a clever gift, fill a cookie jar with these goodies. Using colored paper, cut out a greeting, such as "Happy Birthday." Paste the letters on the cookie jar.

VELVET MASK BALL

1   6-ounce package semisweet chocolate
     morsels
½   cup sugar
¼   cup light corn syrup
¼   cup water
2½   cups finely crushed vanilla wafers (about
     60 wafers)
1   cup unsalted pecans or other nuts
1   teaspoon orange extract
Tinted granulated sugar

Put water in the bottom of a double boiler
and bring to a boil. Put the chocolate morsels
in the top of the double boiler and heat over the
boiling water until melted. Remove from the
heat. Stir in ½ cup of sugar and the syrup. Add
¼ cup water and blend the mixture well.

Put wafer crumbs in a separate bowl. Chop
pecans into very small pieces and mix with the
wafer crumbs. Pour the chocolate mixture in.
Add orange extract and stir well. Shape the
mixture into small balls. Roll each ball in
tinted sugar. Put the gift balls in a covered container. (Nancy uses apothecary jars.) Chocolate balls will keep for several weeks and taste
best after they have "ripened" a few days.

TREASURED TREAT

Add intrigue to your gift balls. Make 1 batch
as the recipe directs. Then make another

batch, substituting butterscotch morsels for the chocolate ones and vanilla flavoring for the orange extract. For a dash of mystery, hide 1 layer of chocolate gift balls under a layer of butterscotch.

WINNING TOASTED NIBBLES

1¼   *pound (5 sticks) margarine or butter*
1   *teaspoon garlic salt*
½   *teaspoon savory salt*
½   *teaspoon celery salt*
6   *teaspoons Worcestershire sauce*
1   *box corn puffs*
1   *box oat puffs*
1   *box bite-sized toasted rice cereal*
1   *pound salted peanuts*
1   *pound can mixed nuts*
1   *small box pretzel sticks*

Heat the oven to 250°.

Put butter in a large roasting pan and slide it into the oven. Let the butter melt and remove the pan. Add salts and Worcestershire sauce. Stir well.

Add cereals, peanuts, and pretzel sticks. Toss well with a fork. Put mixture in the oven and bake for 1 hour and 30 minutes. Stir every 15 minutes while baking.

A GOODY FROM NANCY

Fill holiday tins or attractive glass jars with these super snacks. If you have no container, take an empty cracker or cookie box and cover it with holiday wrapping or other design paper to make your own gift box.

TOMMY'S FRUIT YUMMIES

1   *pound dried apricots*
1   *pound dried pitted prunes*
1   *pound pitted dates*
1   *pound figs*
1   *cup crushed nuts (any kind)*
½ *cup sugar*
Flaked coconut

Grind 1 piece of each kind of fruit at a time into a bowl. Roll spoonfuls of the ground ingredients into candy-sized balls and lay on wax paper. Divide into 4 sections. Roll 1 part in nuts, another in sugar, a third in coconut flakes, and leave the fourth part plain.

SURPRISE STUFFING

Nestle each ball in plastic wrap and form a pretty twist at the top. Place the yummies in

shallow candy boxes, alternating the varieties.
They can be used as Christmas-stocking fillers.

APPLE BUTTER REWARD

12 cups unsweetened applesauce (6 pints or 3
    quarts)
5   cups sugar
½ cup vinegar
1   package crushed cinnamon candy

Put the applesauce, sugar, vinegar, and cinnamon candy in a large saucepan. Stir. Bring the mixture to a boil. Turn heat to medium and cook the apple butter for 25 minutes. The candy will dissolve and the mixture will be thick when the apple butter is done. Remove from the stove and cool until warm.
Makes 6 pints.

SWEET PRIZE

Nancy enjoys buying unusual glass or crockery containers in which to pour her apple butter. She sometimes uses empty jelly, peanut butter, or pickle jars and decorates them with seals to fit the holiday or celebration.

Keep this gift cool, but not refrigerated, until you are ready to give it away.

VANISHING NUT BREAD

½   cup sugar
1   egg
1¼   cups milk
6   ounces chopped pecans
1   cup dates, chopped
3   cups biscuit mix

Heat the oven to 350°.

Put sugar, egg, milk, pecans, and dates in a mixing bowl. Add the biscuit mix. Beat until well-mixed (30 seconds in an electric mixer at high speed).

Grease the sides and bottom of a 9 x 5 x 2½-inch loaf pan. Pour in the mixture. Spread evenly. Bake for 50 minutes. Don't worry if the top of the loaf has a slight crack.

By varying this recipe, you can make Nancy's Christmas Fruit Loaf: Mix 1 cup flour, 1 cup crystallized fruit, and 8 ounces chopped pecans in a bowl. Add sugar, egg, milk, and biscuit mix in the same amounts as the above directs. Stir well. Then follow directions for greasing the loaf pan and baking.

DELICIOUS DUO

Nancy often gives away this delicious fruit loaf in its own aluminum-foil loaf pan and wraps it in colorful cellophane. Or if she bakes both types of loaf, she puts 1 of each into a shoe box which she lines with brightly colored tissue paper and decorates the outside of the box with foil and holiday seals.

COOKING TERMS

Bake Cook in the oven.

Beat Mix fast with beater or spoon.

Blend Mix ingredients until they are smooth.

Boil Cook until liquid is so hot it bubbles hard and steams.

Broil Cook by direct heat. (You can use the broiler section of the oven.)

Brush Spread on the ingredient thinly with a brush.

Chop Cut food in pieces with a knife or chopper.

Combine Mix ingredients together.

Core Remove the stem and seeds.

Cream Beat shortening and sugar until they are well mixed and fluffy.

Cube Cut into ¼- to ½-inch squares.

Dice Cut food into very small cubes.

Dot Drop bits of butter or cheese here and there over the food.

Fold	Mix ingredients gently with a rubber spatula, whisk, or spoon. Cut down through mixture, across the bottom of the bowl, up and over the top, close to the surface of the mixture. Do this over and over.
Fry	Cook in hot fat.
Garnish	Decorate food—for example, a cherry on top of ice cream, or a sprig of parsley on top of potatoes.
Grate	Scrape food against a grater, as in grating a carrot.
Grease	Spread shortening evenly on the bottom and sides of pan.
Melt	Turn butter or margarine into a liquid by heating.
Mince	Chop or cut food into tiny pieces, as in mincing an onion.
Mix	Stir ingredients together.
Pare	Cut away the outside covering of fruits and vegetables.
Peel	Strip off the outer covering, such as peeling a banana.

Pit	Take seeds or pits out of fruit.
Shred	Cut food into very thin strips, such as corned beef.
Sift	Put dry ingredients, such as flour and baking powder, through a sifter or large strainer.
Simmer	Cook food over a very low heat.
Stir	Mix ingredients lightly, such as tossing salad greens.
Whip	Beat eggs and cream with an egg-beater until light and fluffy.

WEIGHTS AND MEASURES

Dash = a small amount (a few grains or a liquid drop)

3 teaspoons = 1 tablespoon

16 tablespoons = 1 cup

4 tablespoons = ¼ cup

8 tablespoons = ½ cup

1 cup = 8 ounces

1 cup = ½ pint

2 cups = 1 pint

4 cups = 1 quart

4 quarts = 1 gallon

½ cup butter = 1 stick or 4 ounces

1 lemon = 3-4 tablespoons juice

Grated peel of 1 lemon = 1 teaspoon

Grated peel of 1 orange = 2 teaspoons

1 square chocolate = 1 ounce

Sizes of Cans:

8-ounce can = 1 cup

#2 can = 2½ cups